Money-Saving Guide to Managing Your Home Remodeling

Money-Saving Guide to Managing Your Home Remodeling

Coleman Volgenau, Jr.

John Wiley & Sons, Inc.

New York • Chichester • Brisbane • Toronto • Singapore

Copyright © 1992 by Coleman Volgenau, Jr.
Published by John Wiley & Sons, Inc.

Library of Congress Cataloging-in-Publication Data:

Volgenau, Coleman, Jr. 1955–
    Money-saving guide to managing your home remodeling / by Coleman
Volgenau, Jr.
       p.   cm.
    Includes index.
    ISBN 0-471-57497-X (pbk.)
    1. Dwellings—Remodeling—Economic aspects. I. Title.
TH4616.V65 1992
643′.7—dc20   91-45785

Printed in the United States of America

10 9 8 7 6 5 4 3 2 1

To my wife, Michelle,
and our three beautiful daughters
for their support, patience, sacrifice, and unconditional love.

Acknowledgments

Inspiration for the writing of this book has come from so many people that it is difficult to know where to begin. Certainly a good place to start is by thanking my mother, Betty Volgenau, whose enduring love, encouragement, and belief in the fulfillment of dreams have always provided a replenishing source for my strength. She may never truly know how much I respect and admire her courage, tenacity, and never-faltering grace. Thank you also goes to my father, Coleman Volgenau, for his love, counsel, and thoughtful influence. A very special thank you to my brother and assuredly my "best man," Peter Volgenau, for his encouragement and support, his enlightened spirit, and his highly valued and appreciated legal counsel. I would also like to thank my father-in-law, Allan W. Hylen, who provided me with much needed technical guidance, who bought me tools, and who provided me with the subtle encouragement to learn how to use them.

All the following people deserve my thanks for their help in the preparation of this book:

A. Scott Bonelli, EA: my old friend, valued confidant, and a talented accountant.

Steve Hester: a friend who inspired many great remodeling ideas.

Francis Klosterman, PA: our trusted accountant and family friend.

Helga Weiss, ASID: a very talented and helpful decorating professional.

Edward Scofield: my dear friend and mentor who taught me how to buy wholesale.

Judge Clarence "Red" Stromwall: my esteemed friend, counselor, and neighbor; the one who advised me to take the pictures.

I would also like to thank all the fine tradesmen and artisans who worked with me and who helped to inspire this book.

Most of all, I would like to thank my wife and our three beautiful daughters for their patience and support throughout the remodeling process and during the writing of this book.

Contents

Appendixes

Money-Saving Guide to Managing Your Home Remodeling

What You Should Know Before Starting the Remodeling Process

S o you have decided to go ahead and do it. You're finally going to make that home of yours into something that you have always dreamed it could be. Your probably need more room, for starters, or maybe you are just tired of jockeying for position with your son or daughter for dibs on that lone bathroom. That electrical wiring needs to be brought up to 1990s standards. Perhaps those old metal water pipes have finally reduced your shower flow to a mere drizzle. Or

Throughout this book, I have used the pronoun "he" and the terms craftsmen and tradesmen to refer nonspecifically to professionals, workers, and other individuals involved in home remodeling. This usage is for convenience only and does not, in any way, imply the exclusion of women from the remodeling business.

have you decided that you really should do something about that kitchen?

Well, now it's time! You've got some great ideas, a little extra money, and all systems are go. But wait—you may not be as prepared as you think you are.

THE NEED FOR A FAMILY PLAN

To borrow a line from a Paul Simon song, it's time to "make a new plan, Stan." Everyone knows you have to have a set of plans, a blueprint to follow, but the architect's drawing is not the plan that I'm referring to. You need a plan for handling this undertaking—the remodeling process. You and your family should sit down and decide just what effect such a building project will have on all of you and just how you "plan" to deal with it. Vacation? Probably not this year. Marital harmony? I wouldn't count on it. Peaceful and relaxing weekends and evenings? Not unless you take my advice and never live at the construction site (more about that later). Even if you don't live at the job site, don't plan on much relaxation.

While most soon-to-be remodelers expect some of these problems, they assume that their family's love and respect for one other will give them the strength and courage needed to weather the storm. At this point, let me explain a very simple truth: *Nothing you have ever done as a family will have prepared you for what you are about to undertake.*

RULES FOR SUCCESSFUL REMODELING

I would like to begin by introducing you to some very basic rules that I have developed for successful remodeling. As you will see, these rules all relate to establishing your "plan" and present a constant theme throughout the book. Remodeling is an orderly "process," and no process can be carried out smoothly and successfully without a workable plan.

Rules for Successful Remodeling

1. Always hire "professionals."

2. Never hire anyone who comes to you looking for work.

3. Always "check" the referrals provided by the workers whom you are considering.

4. Try not to live in your home during a major remodeling.

5. Never plan to have anything done on schedule.

6. Always plan to run at least 20% over budget.

7. Always work "with" your workers and treat them with respect and patience.

Always Hire "Professionals"

Your remodeling project can be a truly rewarding, profitable, and successful experience. The last thing you want is for your project to end in physical or financial disaster because you didn't make the extra effort to hire "professionals."

In Chapter 4, we explore, in depth, the importance of hiring professionals. We will also review the steps you can take to ensure that you are getting the very best and most skilled workers available.

Never Hire Anyone Who Comes to You Looking for Work

This rule does indeed relate to the previous one but there are some very good reasons for making it a separate rule. We will discuss the problems associated with making this mistake in Chapter 4. This type of hiring is more common than you might expect.

Your partially disassembled or unfinished house makes it apparent to all who drive by that you are remodeling. This makes you a potential target for what I call a "we're-working-on-your-neighbor's-house-over-on-the-next-street-and-I-was-just-driving-by, saw-you-were-remodeling, and-thought-maybe-I-could-be-of-service-to-you" subcontractor. Another ploy that I have heard is one in which the homeowner is told: "We just finished up this job and had some materials left over and I can slap a new roof on your place this afternoon for a song." Don't be tempted to do this. They will likely "slap" it on and be cashing your check at your bank before the ink is dry—and before the leaks in your slapped-on roof become evident.

While it is not my intention here to suggest that every subcontractor who approaches you about doing some work is dishonest, you should be cautious about the potential risks. If someone approaches you in this manner and you want to consider the possibility of their involvement in your project, follow the same procedures for checking references as those outlined in Chapter 4.

Always "Check" the Referrals Provided by the Workers Whom You Are Considering

This may seem obvious and I'm sure that you have heard it many times before but the point is crucial: Make the time to do this important task. You certainly don't want to find out halfway through a project that the people you hired were unreliable or incompetent. If you should have to fire a subcontractor and hire another to complete the job, it could end up costing you twice as much—in both time and money—as you had budgeted. Though there certainly is no guarantee that the people you hire after thoroughly checking references will perform to your expectations, you do considerably improve your odds.

In Chapter 4, I will give you some guidelines and a list of questions that you can ask when checking references.

Try Not to Live in Your Home During a Major Remodeling

This rule is particularly important if you have young children. It seems easy to say, "We'll just set up a room for the kids in the dining room" or "We can live, eat, watch television, and let the kids play in the living room because we're not remodeling anything in there." Most tempting of all is the thought of all the money you will save by staying in your home.

While it is true that you may save money, it is also true that you may risk losing your sanity, your marriage, and even—through injury or death—someone you love. Most people think of their home as a sanctuary and their place to escape from the trouble and confusion both in their lives and in the world. This element of security is removed when you begin the remodeling process.

Nothing, I repeat, nothing can prepare you for the intrusion you will experience if you choose to remain in the house. The sound of hammering and sawing, talking, and laughing can all seem so exciting at the start. "This is great . . . just look at the progress we're making," you may find yourself saying after the first few weeks. After the first month or two, however, that enthusiasm will likely change to, "Do they have to turn the water off now? . . . I'm in the shower and I have soap in my eyes." "I had no idea that there would be so much dust!" "And just how do you expect me to cook in 'that' kitchen." "Yes this is Sunday, honey, but it was the only day I could get the tile layer to come." "Well of course the children are cranky, how can they take naps with all 'this' going on!" And, "We want to go outside and play but Mommy says no. She said that one of the men might drop a hammer and hit us on the head!"

While your home is undergoing a major remodeling, move in with friends or relatives if you can, or rent a house or an apartment close to your home. We will discuss ways in which you will be saving money in other areas of your project so that you *can* afford to live elsewhere. I can assure you that it will be money very well spent.

Never Plan to Have Anything Done on Schedule

There's an old axiom about remodeling (and many other things for that matter): "Everything is going to take twice as long and cost twice as much as you expect." For most cases this is an exaggeration, but the basic premise is true. It will undoubtedly take longer to complete each phase of your remodeling project than you expect. The important thing is to be aware of this inevitability so you can properly plan for it. Throughout this book, you will learn more about how to handle and make allowances for this problem.

Always Plan to Run at Least 20% over Budget

To some degree, this rule can be misleading. After all, if we already know that everything may cost as much as 20% more than we budgeted for, why not just add in the 20% factor to each phase of the project when estimating our budget? It may not be that simple. You will need to understand in what areas you are more likely to go over budget and why.

In Chapter 2, I will discuss the topic of budgeting in greater detail and will also provide you with a sample estimate worksheet that you can complete for your own project.

Always Work "with" Your Workers and Treat Them with Respect and Patience

This rule is very important. The old saying that "you can catch more flies with honey than with vinegar" is very true. Your role as manager ("the boss") of the project must include the practice of strong leadership skills.

How can you expect the people who work for you to want to perform to their very best potential if their efforts go unappreciated? You must be willing to learn how to exercise your authority over others in such a way as to instill confidence and draw out loyalty. If your workers believe you are sincerely supportive of their efforts rather than constantly critical of everything they do, they are more likely to perform to your highest expectations. In Chapter 5, you will learn more about how to manage and motivate your workers effectively.

STEP ONE: YOUR FAMILY PLAN

What if, despite your best efforts to make other temporary living arrangements, you end up staying in your home during remodeling. You will need to establish a plan to help you cope. Even if you don't live in your house during remodeling, many of the things discussed here will still apply. Step one of your plan is how to make your sanctuary as livable as possible. Here are some important questions to consider:

1. How will we make our home secure from intrusion by unwanted visitors?

2. How can we make our living area as safe from potential injury as possible?

3. What steps can we take to ensure some degree of privacy?

The first question is often overlooked. Home security has become a greater concern over the last several years. Most people lock their doors and windows before they go to bed or when they are leaving the house. We take it for granted that we *have* doors and windows to lock. During a major remodeling project, it is frequently necessary to remove doors, walls, windows, and roofs. You will need to consider how you will secure your house to protect your belongings and yourselves.

It may be very difficult to protect your home completely under these conditions. There are things you can do, however, to give your family at least a sense of security. One thing that I recommend is to install "temporary" walls, doors, and roofs made out of plywood and 2 by 4 lumber. (Note that builders refer to all "wood products" used to build your home as "lumber" and not "wood." Your subcontractors will be more impressed and perhaps less likely to take advantage of your lack of knowledge if you disguise it by using their terminology.)

You will want to review the blueprints and consult with your subcontractors to determine the best locations for these temporary structures. It may surprise you to discover just how easy it is to work around them. Even if they have to be removed during the workday, they can easily be reset at day's end. You may even wish to install hinges and a padlock on temporary doors that may be opened from the inside of the house. Make sure you consider the ease of escape in the event of a fire. Remember that you just want something that will require more effort and lots of noise to remove if an intruder tries to enter your home. Though these temporary walls and doors will not do much to cut down on the noise and dust during remodeling, they will at least provide both a physical and psychological barrier to the outside world.

The second question regarding safety has several aspects to consider. First and foremost, you should insist that all of your workers be responsible for keeping their work area clean and free from obstructions by the end of each workday. This should be spelled out clearly in all of your contractual agreements. For safety, you should insist that all power tools be unplugged and stored away from where children might have access to them. It would also be a good idea to sit down with your young children and establish boundaries for areas which are off limits to them without your supervision. Children are naturally curious and are bound to want to explore the improved areas. You can satisfy their curiosity by involving them in a nightly tour or review of the day's improvements. Be firm in instructing your children that they may not explore without you. There will be many hazards around your work site that you will all be unaccustomed to.

One hazard that may create a safety concern for infants, young children and pets is old paint. You should be very careful that your child or pet does not ingest old paint chippings that may contain lead. Though modern paints no longer contain lead, the paint in an older home may. This hazard has been known to cause permanent brain damage, so be aware of this danger.

You also need to be aware of asbestos materials that many older houses still contain. This material was commonly used for the insulation of heating ducts and furnaces. You should have a qualified home inspection professional thoroughly inspect your home prior to remodeling to determine if this and/or other potential hazards currently exist in your home. The removal and disposal of this cancer-causing material should only be undertaken by a licensed professional. It can be an expensive undertaking so be sure and budget for it. For a detailed and frank discussion of the hidden health hazards in your home and what you can do to remedy them, I'd recommend reading *Healthy Homes in a Toxic World* by Maury Breecher and Shirley Linde (John Wiley & Sons, 1992).

You can find a licensed home inspection professional by consulting your local yellow pages under the heading "Building & Home Inspection Services." If you are reasonably sure that your home contains asbestos material and if it is practical to have it removed during your remodeling project, consult your yellow pages under "Asbestos Abatement & Removal Service" for a licensed removal contractor in your area. (Also see Appendixes A and C in this book.) You might also contact local realtors to find out who they may recommend. As with all other contractors, be sure to obtain at least three bids because prices will vary. Bear in mind, however, that the Environmental Protection Agency, along with numerous other health organizations, cautions that removing asbestos may represent a greater health hazard than leaving it in place. In any case, always consult with a professional.

Another suggestion that you should consider for your family's safety is to minimize the amount of "things" you retain in your living area. This will cut down on tripping and falling, and allow you to keep escape exits clear in case of fire. You can put all nonessential items into storage during the remodeling. One of the best ways to do this is to lease a storage trailer or bin (sizes vary). They are generally less expensive than public storage yards, and they can be delivered and left at your home. You not only save on the cost of getting the material to and from a storage yard and renting space there, but you always have your possessions "on site" if you should need any of them. They will also remain cleaner and freer of dust and dirt. The storage bins come with a latch device and you can put your own padlock on them. Look in the yellow pages under "Storage." Here again, be sure to call at least three different companies to compare prices.

One item that is a "must have," not only for safety from electrical shock but also to protect your property from water damage, is a plastic tarp sufficient in size to cover the exposed portion of your house. Most additions require some modification of the roof or at least some exposure of the interior walls. The last thing you need is to sustain water damage that could result in additional repair expenses. A 50′ × 100′ plastic tarp is available for around $300 and is cheap insurance when you consider the damage which could be incurred.

One homeowner had their framing contractor temporarily attach a 50 × 100 foot tarp and had it rolled back over the unaffected section of roof. The workers covered the exposed portion at the end of the day if there was even a hint of moisture in the air. One Friday they did not cover the roof. Sunday evening arrived and a 30% chance of rain was predicted. The owners could either gamble on the supposed 70% chance that it would not rain or spend the next hour, in the dark, covering the house with a tarp that weighed about 75 pounds.

They chose to spend the next hour and a half pulling that tarp over the house since they would not have been very safe or effective trying to cover the house in a downpour and when half asleep in the middle of the night. Sure enough, it poured at about 4 AM. The tarp had proved its worth.

The third important question to consider when establishing your plan is that of privacy—specifically, how to retain some modicum of it. Since notions of privacy vary dramatically, consider some very basic ideas.

First, I recommend that you rent some kind of outdoor port-a-john or designate for the workers' use one of the bathrooms that your family will not be using. This will prevent unwanted intrusions into your personal living areas.

Another suggestion for reducing daily disturbances by the workers is to purchase a 5-gallon insulated water jug or thermos. Though most workers bring their own food and beverages, it is a good idea to provide them with ice water and some paper cups. Since most remodeling is done during warm seasons, it is natural that the workers will get thirsty. It doesn't cost you much and you will avoid that frequent question, "Can I get a glass of water?"

Something else to consider may be to establish "off-limits" boundaries for your workers. Most tradesmen and artisans are good about respecting the homeowner's privacy. You are still well-advised, though, to discuss this issue with the workers. Simple courtesies, such as knocking before entering the living area or bathrooms, are obviously important. What about establishing work hours? You are probably not going to appreciate the sound of hammering or the whine of a saw after the children have been put to sleep or before they awake in the morning. You should think ahead of any other do's and don'ts that you want your workers to adhere to. With a little preplanning, you can make the most of a very unprivate experience!

Let's review the things we have discussed in this section by asking and answering the questions we initially raised. Be sure to list any other answers to these questions that you come up with so that you have your own personalized checklist to use.

Checklist for Safety and Privacy

1. How can we make our home secure from intrusion by unwanted visitors?

_____ Review the blueprints and consult with the subcontractor to determine the best location for temporary walls, doors, and roofs.

_____ Have such structures properly installed as the remodeling proceeds.

_____ Others _____

_____ _____

2. How can we make our living area as safe from potential injury as possible?

_____ Insist that subcontractors keep their work area clean and clear from obstructions at the end of each workday.

_____ Ask that all power tools be unplugged and stored daily.

_____ Establish "off-limit" boundaries for the children.

_____ Be aware of the danger of hazardous lead paint chippings around the children.

_____ Have an inspection conducted to determine the presence of asbestos. Have it professionally removed if practical.

_____ Store all unnecessary items away from the living area.

_____ Purchase a plastic tarp to minimize water hazards.

_____ Others _____

_____ _____

3. What steps can we take to ensure some degree of privacy?

_____ Make arrangements to obtain a port-a-john or set aside one bathroom for the workers' use.

_____ Purchase a 5-gallon insulated water jug and some plastic cups for the workers.

_____ Establish "off-limit" boundaries and a list of do's and don'ts for the workers.

_____ Others _____

_____ _____

STEP TWO: FAMILY UNITY

The second step to consider when making your family plan is to decide who speaks for the group. It doesn't matter who is chosen as long as *only one* person interacts on a decision-making level with the workers. This will avoid errors caused by confused signals.

For example, imagine that the following conversation first takes place between "Ward" (the husband) and the plumber:

WARD: Don't you think that it would be better to have the shutoff valves for the washer placed higher on the wall so that it is easier to reach them?

PLUMBER: Well, Ward, your wife said they should be lower so that they can be hidden behind the washer.

WARD: Since June is not here to discuss this, I would like you to put them higher.

Later that same day after the plumber has spent nearly three quarters of an hour raising the shutoff valves, June returns.

JUNE: [to plumber] What on earth are you doing? I told you I wanted those shutoff valves lower!

PLUMBER: Yes I know, June, but your husband told me to put them higher up.

JUNE: I will take this up with Ward but I want you to move them back down again.

You can see the problem associated with having more than one voice: You will drive your workers (and yourselves) crazy and you will waste productive working time. Of course, you will want to discuss things and make decisions based on mutual consent; however, I recommend that you make these decisions *before* directing your workers. Though it is not always possible to discuss all decisions in advance, it is always counterproductive and uncomfortable for your workers to have to deal with dissenting voices.

Family unity also means working together as a "family of ideas" in a spirit of cooperation and sharing throughout the remodeling process. It is important to share and discuss the events that have taken place daily and to explore new ideas and thoughts for the project together. Individual family members will come up with many questions and ideas that should be considered as a group. A number of good, creative ideas can come from this type of free-form discussion.

During one of our projects, my daughter informed me, "Dad, we'll need a night-light in the bathroom." We talked about a $1.49 item at the local drugstore. Another family member suggested that we install one of the recessed lights on its own circuit and hook up a dimmer switch. That way it not only could serve as a night-light by setting the switch very low but at a high setting could also flood the room with light. "How about over the toilet, Dad. That way, I could find my way there without having to wake up you and Mommy." "What a great idea," I said, thinking about avoiding the nightly wake-up call.

In another project, my father suggested we install some switches for the outside floodlights in the upstairs master bedroom. His reasoning was that most people who hear some noise or a disturbance outside their window at night would like to investigate without having to go downstairs or to the front of the house to turn on an outside light. A bedroom switch would make it possible to turn on the floodlights, thus frightening away any possible intruder or, at the very least, providing visibility with minimal effort. Our family took this idea a step further and installed an outside plug for our Christmas lights that was controlled by a switch in the master bedroom as well as by a switch in the downstairs front hallway. This idea was the result of family "brainstorming."

You would be amazed at what you and your family can come up with when you explore new and creative ideas. By exploring the ideas as a family, you will accomplish much more than just coming up with a better idea. It will instill in everyone a strong feeling of participation along with a sense of accomplishment that brings the family closer during a difficult and stressful period.

STEP THREE: DECIDING WHAT TO DO

Now comes the fun part! What do you and your family really want? Do you need a new bedroom for that growing family? What about that new kitchen you have been thinking about? Going to add a bathroom or expand a family room? A new redwood deck off the master suite? What about that den or the playroom for the kids? Are you going to finally finish off that basement? What about that wet bar for entertaining your family and friends?

The first thing that most people will probably say is "Sure I would like to do a lot of things, but the question is can we afford it!" I'm going to get into a more detailed discussion about budgeting and financing in the next chapter, but for now, pretend that money is no object. For this exercise, let your imagination go wild but do remain somewhat practical. (Forget about the indoor pool, the racquetball court, and the bowling alley in the basement unless you are really serious about it!) List all of the realistic remodeling ideas you have been considering.

Once you have your "wish list" for the things you want done, ask yourself some simple questions:

1. How long do we realistically expect to live in this house?

2. If we make the decision to complete the improvements we have conceived, will they be in keeping with the aesthetic flow of our neighborhood?

3. If for some unforeseen reason we should have to sell our home, can we expect to recoup the cost of our improvements?

To some extent, all the questions are interrelated. The first question is probably something you have already thought about. Do you expect to be living in your home for the next 10 to 20 years? Do you intend to pass your home on to your children? Is your employment position reasonably secure and is there little chance that you could be transferred in the future? Even if you can answer yes to all these questions, some caution is in order.

Most American families move, on average, every seven years. The days when people burned their mortgages are, for the most part, a thing of the past. It just doesn't make good economic sense anymore to tie up our home's equity when the money may be put to better use elsewhere. Even if you choose to remodel using your cash reserves rather than borrowing the money, a severe economic downturn, catastrophic illness, or some other unforeseen event could force you to sell your home.

The second question relates to the overall condition of your neighborhood. Do you live in a neighborhood where more and more of the homes are being remodeled and improved? Would you say that the area is showing signs of general improvement or is the neighborhood on the decline? It may not make good sense to make extensive improvements to your home if your next-door neighbors are beginning to let their place go downhill.

To help determine the direction your neighborhood is taking, contact a local realtor and ask for a free market analysis on the value of your home. A realtor can also furnish you with a wealth of other pertinent information. Data on recent home sales along with other general economic and demographic facts are yours for the asking.

Another source for finding the amounts of recent sales of homes in your neighborhood would be your county hall of records. Information on all home sales are in the public domain and are recorded and available for inspection at the county seat.

You can also visit your local building department and inquire about the recent issuance of building permits. You can ask if the number of permits issued represents an upward or downward trend. Armed with this information, you can make a more informed decision about your plans for improvement. If your neighborhood is declining, you should reconsider the extent of your remodeling plans. You wouldn't want yours to be the most expensive and overbuilt house on your block. If this were the case, you might have real trouble selling at your price if you had to. If your neighborhood is in decline, maybe you should even consider buying and remodeling a house in a better area. By doing so, you could get a better return on your remodeling investment dollar.

With respect to the third question—whether or not you can recoup your remodeling investment dollar in the event of a forced sale—you should always give this careful consideration. I have already mentioned the reasons you could be forced to sell. Now we'll attempt to determine a ceiling as to the amount of money you should consider spending while still protecting your investment. This can be very difficult because so many factors affect value, but let's give it a try.

If you have talked to a realtor, you now have a realistic value for your home. For illustration purposes, let's assume that your neighbor just sold a house generally comparable to yours in lot size and location but with a larger floor plan and with more recent improvements. Let's say that he received $225,000 for the sale. The realtor has estimated the value of your unimproved home at $150,000. You now know that you could probably safely spend $75,000 in improvements and still protect your investment (that is, comparable improved home sale price – your home's dollar value = maximum remodeling expenditure). Be aware that this is only one method used to determine how much money you should contemplate spending on a remodeling project. There really are other factors that should also be considered so please be cautious here. Be sure to consider such things as your home's proximity to shopping, where the school district boundaries are drawn, the fiscal effects of your property tax reassessment, and current and/or projected regional and national economic stability. I'm sure that you can come up with some others so take the time to think it through. Always remember that a lot is determined by *how* the money is spent. Try to keep your remodeling ideas consistent with generic tastes. The onyx you put in your foyer may be beautiful, but there is little chance that someone will pay more for your house because you went to the trouble and expense of installing it. Stick to basics, for example, modern functional kitchens with built-ins and bathroom fixtures in neutral colors. It is less risky to express your individuality with accents of color on such easily replaceable items as wallpaper and draperies. Ultimately, of course, the decision as to how much to spend and for what purpose is up to you, but always remember to consider the downside.

Once you have decided just what you want and what is practical for you to have, you can consider how *you* think the changes can be made. What type design would you like to see? You need to answer questions such as these: Where do we want doors and light switches? Do we want just a shower or a bath and shower combined? Where should windows be placed to maximize the morning light but avoid the hot afternoon sun? Will the stove be close enough to the sink and refrigerator? How deep and wide should the counters be? There are many important factors to consider before finalizing your plans. Never be in too big of a rush to begin the project. Give the planning stage adequate time to develop as this may be the single most important phase of your entire project.

It may be helpful to make a list of all of the questions you should ask yourselves. Be creative here, too. Remember, there is no such thing as a stupid question! Again, it would be a good idea to involve the entire family.

Begin to sketch your ideas on paper as if you were looking down at your home without its roof on. Get some graph paper, a ruler, and a soft pencil with a *big* eraser. Have some fun now! It doesn't matter if your drawings don't resemble those of an architect. You are just trying to get clear in your mind what it is that you want. Try to draw your plans to scale using each small square of the graph paper as one square foot of space. You may have to tape several pieces of graph paper together to create an adequate sized sheet.

If you plan to expand the "footprint" of your home, which would require expanding your existing foundation, it is a good idea to sketch the original footprint first and then draw your new area so that you can see if it is really what you want. You may discover that what you want to do could completely change the charm and style of your home and that may not be your intention. Though it is not important to be overly exact in your "fantasy plans," you will find that when you actually commit them to paper, you will want to make changes as you go. When you are finally sure what it is that you want, the plan may have changed completely from your original concept. That's what the eraser is for!

Do not be concerned, at least at this point, with whether or not it is even possible from a structural standpoint to execute what you have drawn. That is what you will hire a professional architect or draftsman and structural engineer for. Just get a feel for what you would be comfortable with.

The best part of this exercise is that, up until this point, you have not had to pay any money for a design. The only thing you have invested is your time. By investing your time and energy, you will save a great deal of money and learn something in the process. I have heard people argue that they just don't have the time to undertake something like this and would rather just hire professionals and not be bothered. These are the same people who usually complain about poor results.

The Architect Versus the Draftsman: Deciding What's Right for You

Most people assume that if they want to have plans drawn up for their remodeling project, they have to talk to an architect (or that your contractor will make arrangements to hire one). Well, at the risk of offending the profession, the advantages of having one draw your plans may not outweigh the cost.

Some architects will charge as much as 15% of the entire cost of the construction project for their services. In this case, the 15% may not be exclusively for drawing the plans. Some of this would be for overseeing the work and ensuring compliance with the drafted plans. This is something you should be able to become capable of doing yourself.

You can consider hiring a draftsman to draw the plans you have specified. A draftsman is someone who may have the talent to be certified as an architect, but lacks the proper credentials or has not as yet completed the necessary school training or apprentice work. Though lacking the experience, such individuals usually make up for this by trying harder to do a good job. The best part of it is that they may charge only 10% to 50% of what it would cost to hire an architect. That's the type of savings we will strive for in this book.

Some people may wonder whether it is "legal" or acceptable to the building department to have someone other than a licensed architect prepare and "certify" your plans prior to submission for approval. In some cases, you may be required to hire a licensed structural engineer to perform "load" and "stress" calculations and certify the plans after you've had your draftsman draw them. You may also be required to have heating, ventilation, and air-conditioning energy calculations certified by a licensed engineer. In California, energy calculations and certification are required under Title 24 of the California Administrative Code. To find out if structural and/or energy calculations and certification are required in your state and on your particular project, contact your city's building department.

Where do you find a competent draftsman? You might ask at the department of architectural studies at a local university or at a nearby community college. You can call that specific department and ask to speak to the department head. Explain what you are looking for and ask if any exceptionally bright students are available who might be able to handle the job. You may be surprised by the enthusiastic response you receive. It may take some time to find just the right person, but the money you save will more than compensate you for your efforts. Another source for finding a draftsman might be your local consumer yellow pages under "Drafting Services." This category can include drafting services that cater to areas other than residential building design so you may have to do a bit of searching.

To locate a certified structural engineer, ask your local building department to recommend one or consult your consumer yellow pages under "Engineers–Civil." You can also call some local architects and ask them whom they use when they need to certify structural calculations. They will often tell you the name of a good civil engineer. These may be engineers who, though working for a large company full time, may enjoy a little free-lance "moonlighting" to earn extra money. I will talk more about the potential savings derived from hiring moonlighters in Chapter 5.

If you should need energy calculations and certification of your plans, consult the yellow pages under "Energy Management & Conservation Consultants." Here too, you can ask the building department or local architects for a recommendation. It may also be well worth your time to go to your public library or the phone company office and obtain a copy of the "Business to Business" yellow pages. Look up draftsmen and engineers under the same categories recommended earlier. During the remodeling process, you may find this particular directory a valuable source for suppliers not listed in the consumer yellow pages.

As with all other suppliers required by your project, prices for architectural and engineering services will vary so be sure to obtain your three estimates.

Now that you have decided what you want to do, you have to determine if you can obtain a building permit for the project.

OBTAINING YOUR BUILDING PERMIT(S)

It is important to clearly understand the procedures involved in obtaining your building permits. People commonly underestimate the time needed to accomplish this important task. As a result, they find themselves frustrated when there are delays in the commencement of the project. To prevent this from happening to you, let's take a closer look at what building permits are and how to go about obtaining them. (See sample building permit, Figure 1–1.)

Why Are Building Permits Necessary?

Building permits and the inspections that accompany them are necessary for three reasons. First and foremost, they are designed to protect and ensure the public safety. Left to their own devices, many people might unintentionally design and construct buildings that are structurally unsound. You certainly would not want your new second story to collapse. Moreover, you wouldn't want to purchase a home that doesn't conform to certain safety standards designed to protect you.

Figure 1–1

Sample Application Form for Building Permit

APPLICATION FOR BUILDING PERMIT

COUNTY OF LOS ANGELES   BUILDING AND SAFETY

FOR APPLICANT TO FILL IN	BUILDING ADDRESS

FOR APPLICANT TO FILL IN

BUILDING ADDRESS

CITY   ZIP

SIZE OF LOT   NO. OF BLDGS. NOW ON LOT

TRACT   BLOCK   LOT NO.

OWNER   TEL. NO.

ADDRESS

CITY   ZIP

ARCHITECT OR ENGINEER   TEL. NO.

ADDRESS

CONTRACTOR   TEL. NO.

ADDRESS   LIC. NO.

CITY   LIC. CLASS

SQ. FT. SIZE	NO. OF STORIES	NO. OF FAMILIES	CHECK ONE
DESCRIPTION OF WORK			NEW ☐
			ADD ☐
			ALTER ☐
			REPAIR ☐
USE OF EXISTING BLDG.			DEMOL ☐

APPLICANT (PRINT)   TEL. NO.

ADDRESS

PRESENT BUILDING ADDRESS

LOCALITY

MOVING CONTRACTOR   TEL. NO.

ADDRESS

REQUIRED SET BACK	YARD	HWY	TOTAL SETBACK FROM PROP. LINE	EXIST. WIDTH
FRONT P.L.				
SIDE P.L.				

P.C. Fee $	Permit Fee
	Issuance Fee
Investigation Fee	Total Fee

BUILDING ADDRESS

LOCALITY

NEAREST CROSS ST.

ASSESSOR MAP BOOK		PAGE	PARCEL

USE ZONE   MAP NO.   SPECIAL CONDITIONS

DISTRICT	GROUP	TYPE CONST.	FIRE ZONE	PROCESSED BY

STATISTICAL CLASSIFICATION		APT.	CONDO.

CLASS NO. _____ DWELL. UNITS _____

SEWER MAP   BK.   PG. _____

VALUATION

$

$

FINAL DATE

FINAL By

VALIDATION

LDMA Ref. #

LDMA P/C #

LDMA Perm. #

SEE REVERSE FOR EXPLANATORY LANGUAGE

Figure 1–1 (continued)

WORKERS' COMPENSATION DECLARATION

I hereby affirm that I have a certificate of consent to self insure, or a certificate of Workers' Compensation Insurance, or a certified copy thereof (Sec. 3800, Lab. C.)

Policy No. _____ Company _____

☐ Certified copy is hereby furnished.

☐ Certified copy is filed with the county building inspection department.

Date _____ Applicant _____

CERTIFICATE OF EXEMPTION FROM WORKERS' COMPENSATION INSURANCE

(This section need not be completed if the permit is for one hundred dollars ($100) or less.)

I certify that in the performance of the work for which this permit is issued, I shall not employ any person in any manner so as to become subject to the Workers' Compensation Laws.

Date _____ Applicant _____

NOTICE TO APPLICANT: If, after making this Certificate of Exemption, you should become subject to the Workers' Compensation provisions of the Labor Code, you must forthwith comply with such provisions or this permit shall be deemed revoked.

LICENSED CONTRACTORS DECLARATION

I hereby affirm that I am licensed under provisions of Chapter 9 (commencing with Section 7000) of Division 3 of the Business and Professions Code, and my license is in full force and effect.

License Number _____ Lic. Class _____

Contractor _____ Date _____

☐ I am exempt under Sec. _____

B.&P.C. for this reason _____

_____ Date: _____

Signature _____

OWNER-BUILDER DECLARATION

I hereby affirm that I am exempt from the Contractor's License Law for the following reason (Section 7031.5, Business and Professions Code):

☐ I, as owner of the property, or my employees with wages as their sole compensation, will do the work and the structure is not intended or offered for sale (Section 7044, Business and Professions Code.)

☐ I, as owner of the property, am exclusively contracting with licensed contractors to construct the project (Section 7044, Business and Professions Code.)

CONSTRUCTION LENDING AGENCY

I hereby affirm that there is a construction lending agency for the performance of the work for which this permit is issued (Sec. 3097, Civ. C.).

Lender's Name _____

Lender's Address _____

I certify that I have read this application and state that the above information is correct. I agree to comply with all County ordinances and State laws relating to building construction, and hereby authorize representatives of this County to enter upon the above-mentioned property for inspection purposes.

_____ _____

Signature of Applicant or Agent   Date

Figure 1–1 (continued)

PLANS TO APPLICANT					INSPECTOR'S NOTES
To:		Returned		Approved	
No.	Date	No.	Date		
Approvals		Required		Date Received or Approved	
		Yes	No		
Water Certificate					
Health Department					
Fire Department					
Grading					
Geological					
Pedestrian Protection (Fence) (Canopy)					
Special Inspection (Conc.) (Masonry) (Welding)					
Lot Drainage					
Parking					
Approvals	Date	Inspector's Signature			
Location— (Setback & Yards)					
Foundations					
Slab					
Frame					
Energy Insulation					
Lath/Drywall— Interior					
Lath—Exterior					
House Number — Correct & Posted					
Final— Enter on Front					

Figure 1–1 (continued)

OWNER-BUILDER DECLARATION

I hereby affirm that I am exempt from the Contractor's License Law for the following reason. (Sec. 7031.5) *Business and Professions Code: Any city or county which requires a permit to construct, alter, improve, demolish, or repair any structure, prior to its issuance, also requires the applicant for such permit to file a signed statement that he is licensed pursuant to the provisions of the Contractor's License Law (Chapter 9) (commencing with Section 7000) of Division 3 of the Business and Professions Code) or that he is exempt therefrom and the basis for the alleged exemption. Any violation of Section 7031.5 by any applicant for a permit subjects the applicant to a civil penalty of not more than five hundred dollars ($500).):*

☐   I, as owner of the property, or my employees with wages as their sole compensation, will do the work, and the structure is not intended or offered for sale (Sec. 7044) *Business and Professions Code: The Contractor's License Law does not apply to an owner of property who builds or improves thereon, and who does such work himself or through his own employees, provided that such improvements are not intended or offered for sale. If, however, the building or improvement is sold within one year of completion, the owner-builder will have the burden of proving that he did not build or improve for the purpose of sale).*

☐   I, as owner of the property, am exclusively contracting with licensed contractors to construct the project (Sec. 7044) *Business and Professions Code: The Contractor's License Law does not apply to an owner of property who builds or improves thereon, and who contracts for such projects with a contractor(s) licensed pursuant to the Contractor's License Law).*

☐   I am exempt under Sec. _____ , B.&P.C. for this reason _____

Date _____ Owner _____

INSPECTOR'S NOTES

_____

_____

_____

_____

_____

_____

_____

_____

_____

_____

_____

_____

The second reason for having permits and inspections is to protect you and your investment from the idiosyncrasies of your neighbors. Let us assume that your next-door neighbor gets an urge to construct an 18-foot concrete and barbed wire fence along the property line surrounding his or her home. Or worse yet, maybe a neighbor who is a modern artist decides to construct a monolith 65 feet in height that obstructs your view of the lake. You could be devastated both psychologically and financially. To prevent this, everyone must follow established guidelines, commonly known as the Uniform Building Code™ in the Western region of the United States (see Appendix E). Properly issued building permits and their resulting inspections accomplish this objective.

The third reason for obtaining permits is to protect you after you have sold your home. In some states, you will be required to disclose any alterations you have made that change the structure of your home. Failure to do so may make you liable for any incorrect alterations that may result in injuries or damages to the person who buys your home. The building permit and inspection process ensures that you have done things correctly and in accordance with acceptable standards.

When Are Building Permits Unnecessary?

In some cases, you may not be required to obtain a building permit. Such things as above-ground swimming pools, fences less than 6 feet in height, a toolshed, your children's playhouse, or wood moldings and interior decorations may be exempt from the permit process. You should certainly check with your local building department in advance to find out what is and what is not exempt.

How to Obtain the Required Permits

Every municipality or county government has a building department of some kind. Consult your telephone book under the government listing section for the Building and Safety Department; Department of Construction; Department of Building Permits and Inspections; Department of Land Use and Zoning; Construction Department; or Department of Licenses. Depending on where you live, it may be called by different names. Visit the corresponding department in your area to obtain published information on how to apply for a permit and the rules governing building code compliance (see also Appendix D).

You may need to visit different departments for various phases of your project. For example, you may be required to contact and obtain permits from your county's health department if you plan to install a new sewage system. Be sure to ask for guidance at your building department as to what other departmental approvals may be required. These people are there to help you, so don't hesitate to enlist their assistance.

The project you intend to undertake also may require some kind of "variance" that will force you to apply for an exception to the established zoning regulations. Such things as a divergence in setback, height, and easement restrictions are all examples of issues that may require you to apply for a variation.

This request for a variation procedure could require you to do no more than obtain approval from the Director of Community Development or the person holding the equivalent post. Other applications for a variance can involve much more substantial and time-consuming procedures. These may force you to obtain the consent of your neighbors in the community, to obtain the signatures of your immediate neighbors in the form of a "Notice of Intent" petition; and/or to publish a notice in your local newspaper. Furthermore, this formal process could necessitate public hearings and a council vote to grant you permission on the variance. All these things can force a delay in the approval of your plans. Additionally, you stand a better-than-average chance that the community will deny your request entirely. By being aware of these regulations and restrictions early in your planning stages, you will be better prepared to manage your time, efforts, and expenditures accordingly.

The physical process of applying for your building permit involves your becoming familiar with what will generally be required. You can expect that along with the completed application (see Figure 1–1), you will need to submit at least two complete sets of blueprints or construction plans for your project. These plans should be very detailed and must show the existing floor plan along with the proposed additions; all building dimensions, framing cross sections and foundational support structures along with their corresponding details and specifications; all exterior elevations and roof details; all hardware and lumber specifications; and all electrical outlets, switches, and lights. You will also need to provide a plot plan showing the location of your home's proposed "footprint" and its relationship to the lot size. These plans should also include such things as the structural and/or energy calculations if necessary.

If you plan on being the owner-builder and directly employing all subcontractors for your project, it may also be necessary for you to provide proof of workmen's compensation insurance along with your application.

For your own protection, you will want to be sure to carry such insurance as well as liability coverage anyway. (I will talk more about this in the next chapter.)

How Much Will the Permit Cost?

Along with your completed application and copies of your plans, you will be required to pay some fees. You can expect to pay fees to cover such items as the permit itself along with an issuance fee and perhaps some local school impact fees. The cost of these items will be determined by the increased square footage multiplied by an established factor. For example, if your plans called for you to add 1,200 square feet to your home and the valuation factor was $55 per square foot, your new valuation would be $65,000 (1,200 × 55 = 65,000). This means that your home's assessed value would increase by $65,000. This number would then be used to calculate your permit fee and assess your school impact fees. The factor used will vary depending on where you live so be sure and have the building department explain how they make their calculations. Don't confuse these fees with the assessment of your property taxes. Your local tax assessor will automatically be notified of your improvement plans through the permit procedure. You can most likely expect a reassessment of your improved property and to pay more in annual property taxes.

In some locations, you may have to post a completion bond providing insurance that your project will be completed as planned. This bond will take the form of having the building department hold a money deposit until the project is complete and the final inspections have been made and approved. Here again, be sure to ask the building department if this is necessary for your particular project.

How Long Will It Take to Obtain Plan Approval and Receive the Permit?

Obtaining plan approval will vary depending on the extent of the work to be done and just how busy or backlogged the department may be. Simple projects such as upgrading the electrical, plumbing, sewers, and roofing; remodeling kitchens and bathrooms without structural changes; and installing new cement driveways and walkways do not require extensive approval procedures. These permits can generally be issued at the same time that you apply for them. More extensive remodeling projects requiring new foundations and footprint extensions can take anywhere from a few weeks to a few months. Plan approval involving second-story additions and extensive structural alterations and those requiring the variances, which we have already discussed, can take anywhere from a few months to as long as a year. Be sure to ask the building department to estimate how long they think approval may take and plan accordingly.

When and How Will the Inspections Occur?

If you intend to function as the owner-builder, it will be your responsibility to schedule and call for the periodic inspections that will be required. Don't allow the prospect of having to do this frighten you because, once again, you will not be operating in a vacuum. You should instruct your subcontractors to tell you when they have completed their required tasks and are ready for you to call for inspection.

Depending on the extent of your project, you will be required to call for inspections at two phases during the course of your remodeling. The first will be immediately after completion of the rough phases. The second will be at the final inspection phase when your project has been completed.

The rough inspections will be conducted after the forms for your new foundation footings have been built and before any concrete has been poured; after all rough framing has been completed including fire stops, braces, hold downs, bolts, straps, and other framing as required by your plans and before these walls have been covered by drywall or other siding or coverings; after your drywall has been "nailed" in place and before the joints have been sealed; after your lath is in place on either interior or exterior walls but before any plaster or stucco has been applied; after all rough wiring has been installed and prior to the installation of fixtures or the final connections to the power; after all forced-air heating units, air conditioning, boilers, vents, and ducts have been placed in approved locations with allowances made for proper clearance and access; after all rough plumbing has been installed and tested for leaks and proper ventilation and before the fixtures have been connected; and after septic tanks, cesspools, and/or leach fields have been dug and installed and before they have been covered. (See sample inspection record, Figure 1–2.)

The final inspection, as already mentioned, will be conducted after all the "finish" work has been completed in a satisfactory manner for the applicable items. At this point, the building inspector will "sign off" on

Figure 1–2

Sample Inspection Record Card

POST THIS CARD AT JOB SITE

INSPECTION RECORD
PERMITS WILL BE VOIDED IF WORK IS
STOPPED FOR 180 CONSECUTIVE DAYS

BLDG. PERMIT NO.	DATE	GROUP

ADDRESS

OWNER

NOTE: *Do Not Cover Walls Until Frame, Insulation, Electrical, Mechanical and Plumbing Have Been Signed.*

BUILDING	DATE	INSPECTOR'S SIGNATURE
FOUNDATION: LOCATION FORMS, SETBACK		
SLAB		

Pour No Concrete Until Above Has Been Signed

	DATE	INSPECTOR'S SIGNATURE
FRAME: FIRE STOPS, BRACING, BOLTS		
INSULATION		
LATH. INT. ☐ DRYWALL ☐		
LATH. EXT.		

ELECTRICAL	DATE	INSPECTOR'S SIGNATURE
UNDER SLAB WORK		
ROUGH CONDUIT		
ROUGH WIRING		
TEMP. POWER		

MECHANICAL	DATE	INSPECTOR'S SIGNATURE
FAU A.C. REF BOILER OTHER		
COMBUST. & CIRCULAT. AIR, DUCTS, VENTS, ETC.		
LOCATION, CLEARANCE, ACCESS		

PLUMBING	DATE	INSPECTOR'S SIGNATURE
UNDER SLAB WORK		
ROUGH PLUMBING		
ROUGH GAS PIPING		
HOUSE SEWER		
SEPTIC TANK, SEEP PIT(S) AND/OR DRAINFIELD		

FINAL APPROVALS	DATE	INSPECTOR'S SIGNATURE
ELECTRICAL		
GAS PIPING		
MECHANICAL		
PLUMBING FIXTURES		
BUILDING		

the inspection report and "close out" the permit. It is not necessary to call for the final inspection until everything is done but you should be aware of the time restrictions governing the project's completion. In Los Angeles County, for example, the permit becomes void if work has stopped for longer than 180 consecutive days. If you allow the permit to lapse, you may be required to reapply and pay additional fees to resume the work. Be sure that you are aware of the time restrictions for your particular location and plan accordingly.

REVIEW

- Review the rules for successful remodeling.

- Develop your family's plan for your project and think about safety, security, and privacy.

- Consider where you plan to put temporary walls and doors.

- Plan to eliminate potential hazards such as lead paint and asbestos.

- Consider hiring a professional home inspection consultant.

- Consider renting a storage container for your belongings.

- Purchase a plastic tarp for protection from wet weather.

- Consider toilet facilities for your workers.

- Purchase a 5-gallon water jug for use by your workers.

- Establish boundaries and a set of rules for your workers to follow.

- Decide who will interact with the workers in making decisions.

- Work together with your family in developing ideas for the project.

- Consider the likelihood of a move in your future and plan your project to adhere to common tastes.

- Investigate the growth and development of your neighborhood so that you can plan to recoup your remodeling investment dollar when you do sell your home.

- Draw your plans yourself first to be clear on what you want to do.

- Consider hiring a draftsman rather than an architect for substantial savings.

- Contact your local building department for information on obtaining permits.

- Find out how much your permits will cost.

- Find out about how long it will take to obtain your plan approval and permits.

- Understand at what point inspections will occur and how to request them.

How to Estimate Costs and Build Your Remodeling Budget

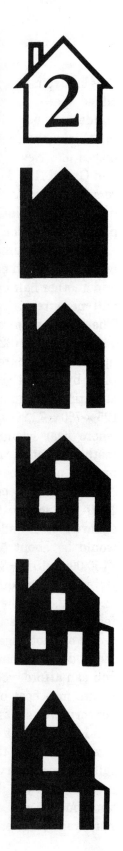

By now you should have a pretty good idea what you want to have done. You have preliminarily discussed your conceptual plans with a draftsman (or architect if you prefer) and are comfortable with the direction you intend to take. The problem now is cost. Here I will explain how to estimate the costs of each phase of the project and plan your budget accordingly.

JUST HOW MUCH IS ALL THIS GOING TO COST?

Throughout the country, I have heard contractors throw around actual building cost figures ranging from $85 per square foot to as much as $150 per square foot of added space. As you can see, that is a pretty big spread. The figure a builder will use will vary depending on what part of the country you live in. Obviously these per-square-foot building costs will be higher in places like New York and Los Angeles, and much lower in Des Moines and Grand Rapids. These numbers are designed to give a general idea of remodeling costs, but they really don't mean very much when you get down to formulating a specific budget after you have completed your plans. Your actual costs are influenced by so many different factors.

Let us assume that you plan to add a new wing onto your existing home, which will contain a new master suite, a family room with wet bar, and another half bathroom. The master suite, which includes a bathroom, will measure out at 20 by 16 feet, yielding 320 square feet ($20 \times 16 = 320$). The family room and adjoining half bath will measure 22 by 20 feet, or 440 square feet ($22 \times 20 = 440$). By combining the square footage, we come up with 760 square feet of addition ($320 + 440 = 760$). Using a figure, supplied by a local general contractor, of $95 per square foot for new construction, we can estimate a total of approximately $72,200 for our project ($95 \times 760 = 72,200$). But what does this number really mean? Is this anywhere near what our project will finally end up costing? Using this method of estimating building costs could wind up forcing you to cut back on your project because of budget constraints.

In one project, the architect told the owner to expect to pay about $150 per square foot for a second-story addition consisting of 1,000 square feet. By adding the architect's fee of 15% of the job, the estimate would be about $172,500 for the whole project ($150/sq. ft. $\times$ 1,000 = $150,000 $\times$ 15% = $22,500 + $150,000 = $172,500). That brought the projected cost per square foot to approximately $172.50 ($172,500 ÷ 1,000 sq. ft. = $172.50). That was entirely too much money for only 1,000 square feet of added space.

I am not suggesting that you should completely dismiss the general method of estimating on a per-square-foot basis. In determining what you can afford, you have to have some rough idea of what your improvements may cost before you can order your plans drawn. If by using a conservative square footage estimate you discover that you are way beyond your budget constraints, you may need to scale down the project's size. If you find that you can accomplish everything you plan and still fall within or very close to your budget, by all means order your drawings. Should you discover, by using this method, that you have exceeded your budget and still wish to determine if your project is feasible, you may want to invest the money for your drawings and complete the estimating exercise. After you have obtained all your numbers and have made some allowances for going over budget (to be discussed later in this chapter), you can then determine if it will be necessary to scale down your plans. The problem in doing this is that you will have to retrace your steps and reestimate everything according to the new design. You can also expect additional costs for drawing the revised plans.

You will need detailed plans before you can obtain accurate estimates for many phases of the proposed project. Your final numbers should come in at less than the estimate if you have done your homework and have saved money in the areas in which you feel comfortable doing the work yourself.

THE PROCESS OF PHYSICALLY ESTIMATING YOUR COSTS

What numbers should you use to estimate your actual building and design costs? Figure 2–1 provides an actual Contractor's Estimate Sheet prepared by Wolcotts, Inc. This form should be available at your local office supply or stationery store. If it is not in stock, ask the stationer to order one for you. Although some of the items on this sheet will pertain only to new construction, it is an excellent reference tool for the remodeler as well. Feel free to alter the estimate sheet to conform to your use if you discover that there are not specific "slots" available to "plug" in your estimates. The necessity to do this will become more apparent to you in the following discussion.

Although you may fill in the pertinent information on this sheet in any order, for discussion purposes we will walk through each phase on a priority basis. (See Figure 2–1.) One of the most difficult responsibilities you will have as an owner-builder will be the proper scheduling and managing of the various tradesmen. It is therefore important for you to approach the project with a thorough understanding of the order in which each phase will take place. Knowing what comes next will save you time and money when your project finally gets underway. Chapter 5 provides a more thorough discussion of scheduling.

Plans, Specifications, and Engineering

Assuming that by now you have found a draftsman you feel comfortable working with, he should be able to give you a pretty firm price for

Figure 2-1

Sample Estimate Sheet

CONTRACTOR'S ESTIMATE SHEET

Location _____ Lot _____ Block _____ Tract _____

Owner _____ Address _____ Phone _____

Architect _____ Address _____ Phone _____

Description _____ Size _____ Sq. Ft. _____ Started _____ Comp. _____

Architectural
Plans & Specifications _____ $_____
Engineering _____ $_____

Preliminary
Survey _____ $_____
Wrecking _____ $_____

Legal
Building Permit _____ $_____
Water Tap _____ $_____
Street Deposit _____ $_____
Construction Water _____ $_____

Excavating
Exc. _____ yds. @ _____ $_____
Grading & Filling _____ $_____
Hauling _____ $_____

Concrete
Walls, etc. _____ cu. ft. @ _____ $_____
Reinforcing Steel _____ $_____
Walks, etc. _____ sq. ft. @ _____ $_____
Floors _____ sq. ft. @ _____ $_____
Steps _____ lin. ft. @ _____ $_____
Curbs _____ lin. ft. @ _____ $_____
Misc. _____ $_____

Masonry
Common Brick _____ M @ _____ $_____
Hollow Tile _____ M @ _____ $_____
Chimneys & Fireplace _____ $_____
Mantels _____ $_____
Stone Work _____ $_____
Face Brick _____ M @ _____ $_____

Lumber
Rough _____ M @ _____ $_____
Finish _____ M @ _____ $_____

Carpentry
Rough _____ $_____
Finish _____ $_____

Sanitation
Plumbing _____ $_____
Sewer _____ $_____
Cesspool _____ $_____

Metal Work
Structural Steel _____ $_____
Sheet Metal _____ $_____
Ornamental Iron _____ $_____
Steel Sash _____ $_____

Roof
Composition _____ $_____
Tile _____ $_____
Trusses _____ $_____
Misc. _____ $_____

Lath & Plastering
Exterior _____ yds. @ _____ $_____
Interior _____ yds. @ _____ $_____
Staff Work _____ $_____
Misc. _____ $_____

Hardware
Rough _____ $_____
Finish _____ $_____
Misc. _____ $_____

Electrical
Wiring _____ $_____
Fixtures _____ $_____

Heating
Gas _____ $_____
Misc. _____ $_____

Mill Work
Frames _____ $_____
Interior Finish _____ $_____
Sash _____ $_____
Doors _____ $_____
Screens _____ $_____
Cabinets _____ $_____
Stair Work _____ $_____
Ironing Boards _____ $_____
Misc. _____ $_____

Glazing
Misc. Glass _____ $_____
Plate Glass _____ $_____
Mirrors _____ $_____
Corner Beads _____ $_____
Weather Strips _____ $_____

Tile
Tile Work _____ $_____
Mantels _____ $_____
Misc. _____ $_____

Painting & Decorating
Paint Material _____ $_____
Paint Labor _____ $_____
Wall Paper & Labor _____ $_____
Special Decorating _____ $_____
Waterproofing _____ $_____

Floors
Hardwood _____ yds. @ _____ $_____
Linoleum _____ yds. @ _____ $_____
Composition _____ $_____

Miscellaneous
Window Shades _____ $_____
Curtain Rods _____ $_____
Awnings _____ $_____
Wall Beds _____ $_____
Incinerator _____ $_____
Refrigeration & Ice Boxes _____ $_____
Insulation & Deadening _____ $_____
Cleaning Windows, etc. _____ $_____
Removing Debris _____ $_____

Landscaping
Lawn _____ $_____
Shrubbery _____ $_____
Sprinkler System _____ $_____
Fence _____ $_____
Drainage _____ $_____

Insurance
Compensation _____ $_____
Liability _____ $_____
Fire _____ $_____
Bond _____ $_____

Extras
_____ $_____
_____ $_____
_____ $_____
_____ $_____

TOTAL COST _____ $_____
PROFIT _____ $_____
COMPLETE BID _____ $_____

architectural services. Talking to the building department and to your draftsman should enable you to find out whether you will need a structural or other engineer to certify your plans. You should also have little difficulty obtaining a price from these professionals.

Enter your estimates for these items under "Architectural" on the Contractor's Estimate Sheet.

Building Permit

In Chapter 1, we talked about going to the building department to obtain some general guidelines for building permit costs, such as the actual permit fee, an issuance fee, and some school taxes. After providing the building department representative with the approximate total square footage of your planned improvement, he or she will be able to determine a fairly accurate figure for the cost of your permit. You will also discover what other permits may be required, and you can obtain costs for them as well. Enter these estimates under "Legal" on the estimate sheet.

Insurance

As owner-builder, it is critical for you to review your homeowner's insurance with your agent to find out if your policy includes coverage for workmen's compensation and extended liability. Also find out what additional coverage you may need if you choose to live away from the project site and whether the building materials lying around your job site are covered under your policy as well. If you do not have coverage for these items and if it is available to you, I strongly urge you to consider adding it for the duration of your remodeling project.

Although most subcontractors you will hire carry workmen's compensation on the people they employ, anyone who is not covered may come looking to you in the event of an accident. Be sure to obtain costs for this added insurance coverage and list it on the estimate sheet under "Insurance."

Temporary Storage

As discussed in Chapter 1, contact your three storage bin suppliers, make your price inquiries, and enter your cost in the "Extras" section.

Temporary Housing

In Chapter 1, I recommended that you avoid living in your home during a major remodeling project. If you do plan to move elsewhere for the duration of the project, you are going to need to budget for temporary housing. Give some thought to where you plan to go and investigate the costs involved. You may discover that an apartment or rental house would be suitable for your needs. Make some inquiries through a local realtor or your newspaper to determine how much you should have to pay for this housing.

Depending on the extent of your project, you should plan to arrange for a place to live for from six months to one year. I would not recommend signing a long-term lease (one year or longer); it is preferable to rent on a month-to-month basis with the right to provide 30 days' notice prior to vacating. This arrangement will protect your right to move out as your remodeling progress dictates.

Enter your estimate for temporary housing under the "Extras" section of your Contractor's Estimate Sheet.

Wrecking (Demolition)

Your project will undoubtedly involve some sort of demolition. If you plan to add any space to your home or even if you are planning just to redo an area within your existing structure, it will require some destruction and removal of debris. The extent to which this may be necessary is something you should discuss with your draftsman and framing contractor.

Some contractors specialize in residential demolition. You can find them by asking some of the sources previously discussed or by consulting the yellow pages under "Demolition Contractors." While this is one area where you may be able to save a great deal of money by doing it yourself, I do recommend that you at least obtain costs from the contractors for estimating purposes. Be sure to enter these numbers onto the Contractor's Estimate Sheet. It never hurts to estimate on the high side, even if you plan to do it yourself for greater savings.

If you should decide that you want to tackle the demolition phase without the aid of a contractor's labor force, you might want to consider hiring your own day laborers to assist with this messy task. If you have trouble locating day workers in your area, you could notify your local unemployment office and solicit its services in finding people. You might also contact your local high school or college student employment assistance office and ask for help in hiring some hard-working students.

If you hire these day laborers and pay them in cash, be sure and purchase a receipt book at your local stationery store so that you can keep an accurate record of your expenditures. Plan on spending about $5 to $7.50 per hour for each worker you hire. It would be wise to have these day laborers complete an IRS Form W-9, which will provide you with their address and social security numbers. At the end of the year you may then present them with an IRS Form 1099 clearly demonstrating the total amount that you have paid them. This documentation will be particularly important if you employ the laborers for an extended period. You will discover that it is important not only to produce receipts but to substantiate these expenditures if you should be audited by the IRS after you sell your home. Be sure to check with your accountant about the feasibility of doing this. The forms will be available from the accountant or your local IRS office. In Chapter 7, I will explain more thoroughly how remodeling affects the tax issues governing the sale of your home.

A word of caution here. You will want to be very careful that you and your demolition laborers clearly understand what needs to be removed. The last thing you would want is to destroy something unnecessarily, which could increase your costs and maybe even delay your project. Make sure that you are available to properly supervise the work being done.

Enter your estimated costs for wrecking under the "Preliminary" section of your estimate sheet.

Removing Debris

This responsibility is closely linked to your demolition phase. In estimating the previous category, we included the cleanup costs under labor, but some way of containing and removing the debris is also necessary. For this you will need to obtain costs for one or more large trash bins that can be brought in and left at your job site while you complete your cleanup. Various sizes are available, depending on the amount of debris that you will need to have removed, and prices will vary for equivalent-sized trash bins so do obtain at least three bids. You will find that you may need more than one container and at different times throughout your project. Some suppliers may charge a premium for leaving the bins at your job site for longer than seven days, so be sure to ask about that. Trash removal companies are listed in the consumer yellow pages under "Rubbish Containers & Hauling." If the company offers a contractor's discount for this service, by all means, take advantage of it.

If your job is relatively small and you plan on hauling the debris to the dump in your own truck, estimate the number of trips you might need and the cost to dump each load. You may also want to factor in the cost of your gasoline.

Enter your estimated costs for debris removal under "Miscellaneous" on the Contractor's Estimate Sheet.

Excavating

This is another area where you could save some money by doing it yourself or by hiring day laborers. If your project involves extending the present footprint of your home or if your old foundation will require additional footings to support a second story, it may be worth your energies to organize the labor and supervise the digging effort. This would be particularly true if the area needing excavation is not readily accessible to heavy machinery and a contractor's own labor force would be required for the work. In that case, you could expect to pay a premium.

I do not recommend that you hire your own labor for substantial work. Should your plans call for digging a basement or a swimming pool, you would obviously be better off in hiring a heavy equipment contractor for the excavation.

As with all phases of your project, I do recommend that you obtain contractors' costs for estimating purposes. Here again, if you can save money by doing the work yourself, more power to you. It is just a good idea to cover yourself against cost overruns in other areas by estimating on the high side.

Concrete (Foundation Work)

Here you should deal strictly with the actual cost of having the forms built, the concrete poured, and finish work completed on the foundation only. Later on, I will discuss driveways, walkways, or other areas that may require concrete.

Because foundations must adhere to the very detailed specifications outlined in your blueprints, I do not recommend that you attempt to form, pour, and finish your concrete footings yourself. Because of its quick setting properties, concrete can be difficult to work with. Unless you have plenty of experience, leave this task up to a professional concrete contractor. Obtain your three bids, ask for references (see Chapter 4), and select the contractor that you feel most comfortable with. Remember to have your foundation forms inspected by the building inspector prior to pouring the concrete. If you fail to order an inspection and the concrete is poured incorrectly, the building department could force you to redo it. It is certainly not worth taking that risk.

To enter your estimate, find the "Concrete" section of the Contractor's Estimate Sheet.

Carpentry (Rough)

Your framing contractor will handle rough carpentry. These professionals build the skeletal wood framing of your remodeling project and will follow your plans accordingly. As necessary, they will build and erect the exterior or "exposed" walls, partitions, or interior walls; they will rough frame all doors and windows; install all joists, posts, headers, beams, rafters, sheathing, subflooring, and sills; and will rough frame your staircase.

In some cases, the same contractor may do your finish carpentry too. For estimating purposes, the contractor should break out the costs for rough framing and finish carpentry separately. Don't agree to a package deal unless you feel really comfortable with his work or the combined estimate is too good to pass up. You want the option of being able to replace the subcontractor, after completion of the rough carpentry phase, if you are not entirely satisfied with his general work.

List these costs under "Carpentry–Rough."

Lumber (Rough)

This area may require a little practice to estimate accurately, but remember that you are not operating inside a vacuum. Ask the rough framing subcontractor you plan on hiring to make a list of necessary materials. Some lumberyards will also be willing to estimate the materials that are required. Just show the customer service representative the plans and he should be able to give you a pretty accurate cost estimate. Enter this figure on your estimate sheet under "Lumber–Rough."

Hardware (Rough)

Hardware for the rough framing includes such items as anchor bolts, joist hangers, hold downs, various sizes of nails and wood screws, straps, and any other steel or metal items that may be required. These hardware items are also available from your lumberyard or local building supply store. You should be able to obtain quantities and estimates by talking with your subcontractor, draftsman, and/or supplier. Enter the costs under "Hardware–Rough."

Masonry (Rough)

This category includes projects requiring a brick or stone fireplaces and/or mantels and face brick for home siding. If your plans require these materials, you will need to obtain estimates both for material and labor. To determine labor costs, contact subcontractors who specialize in masonry work and obtain three estimates. For material costs, talk with your subcontractor, your draftsman, and your material supplier to determine how much will be needed. These numbers should be entered on your estimate sheet under "Masonry."

Plumbing (Rough)

On the Contractor's Estimate Sheet, plumbing can be listed under "Sanitation." Divide the plumbing estimate into two parts, "rough" and "finish." In keeping with proper procedural order, let's deal exclusively with rough plumbing first.

    This category could even be subdivided into sections for labor and material, but it is usually easier to have the plumbing contractor provide his own material. The time that you could spend obtaining material estimates may not outweigh the savings. Unless you are planning to repipe your entire home, have the plumber include rough material costs along with labor in the estimate. Your opportunity to obtain your own costs for materials will come in the finish plumbing phase when you should purchase all your actual plumbing fixtures.

Sewer/Cesspool

Adding bedrooms and/or bathrooms to your home may require updating your sewage disposal system. If you are already on sewers, it may only be necessary to have your plumber hook into the existing sewer line. If you are on septic tanks, cesspools, or other types of sewage systems, you may have to update or expand your current system. In any case, contact your building department to find out what your plans may require. If necessary, ask the building department or other available sources to recommend a qualified specialist in this field. You may also consult the yellow pages under "Septic Tanks & Systems" to find a local licensed contractor. Follow through by obtaining your three bids (see Chapter 4) and enter the estimate under "Sanitation."

Heating (and Air Conditioning)

If your plans include increasing the size of your home, you may need to extend or expand your heating and, if applicable, your air-conditioning system. This may involve something relatively simple, such as extending the air ducting to the improved area. It may also require the more complex (and more expensive) task of upgrading your entire system by either adding additional service equipment or replacing the system currently in use. In either case, you will need to obtain estimates from heating and air-conditioning contractors. Follow the procedures already discussed and enter your estimates in the "Heating" section of your Contractor's Estimate Sheet.

Electrical (Rough Wiring)

Here is another area where you can experience huge savings by doing some of the rough (and finish) work yourself. It makes sense to have some reservations about dealing with electricity—having been "zapped" by electrical current a couple of times in my youth, I have always had a healthy respect for it and the professionals who dare to work with it. But to assist in rewiring, you don't have to have a complete understanding of how it all works. What you do need is a lot of wire and someone to "run" it through the walls. You would be surprised at how quickly you can learn to do this with the proper guidance.

For this plan to be feasible, I recommend hiring a first class, "moonlighting" licensed electrician (see Chapter 5), who will direct and handle most of the actual hook-up work. You will simply assist and be his "gopher."

If you feel comfortable in handling the electrical phase of your project yourself or if you can locate a cooperative licensed electrician the savings can be substantial. Of course, not all electricians are enthusiastic about working with an inexperienced person. You may have to do some searching to find one who will endorse your plan.

Obtaining the required electrical permit from the local building department is customarily done by the electrical contractor who handles the job. If you decide to do the work, you will be the person responsible for completing the application and obtaining the permit. This is not difficult to do. Simply count the number of plug receptacles, lighting, and switch outlets along with the expected number of lighting fixtures or other power apparatus, large appliances or service panels indicated on your plans and enter them in the spaces provided on the application. (See Figure 2–2.) If you have questions about the application, be sure to ask for assistance from the building department or from the licensed electrician with whom you intend to do the work.

To complete the estimating sheet, obtain your estimates for the rough electrical work from three subcontractors. Even if you end up not using them, you will have a pretty good idea of what it should cost. Although you may save by doing some of the work yourself, it is better to use a contractor's cost to protect yourself in other areas where you may go over budget. Enter this estimate on your estimate sheet under "Electrical–Wiring."

Sheet Metal

This involves such features as the metal flashing around a chimney, skylight, window, or any other place with a potential for water leaks. It may also include ventilation ductwork or hoods. Installation of rain gutters

Figure 2–2

Application for Electrical Permit

20-0019 DPW 9/89
76A663

APPLICATION FOR ELECTRICAL PERMIT

COUNTY OF LOS ANGELES   DEPT. OF PUBLIC WORKS   BUILDING AND SAFETY DIV.

FOR APPLICANT TO FILL IN	EACH	NO.	FEE		JOB ADDRESS		
New Residential Bldgs. & Pools					LOCALITY		
1 & 2 -Family, Sq. Ft. _____	$	—	$				
Multi-family Sq. Ft. _____		—			NEAREST CROSS ST.		
Residential Swimming Pools					ASSESSOR MAP BOOK	PAGE	PARCEL
Outlets: Rec. ___ Light ___ Sw. ___					OWNER OR FIRM NAME		
First 20					MAIL ADDRESS		
Total No. _____ Additional					CITY	Tel. No.	
Lighting Fixtures First 20					PLAN CHECK APPLICANT		
Total No. _____ Additional					ADDRESS		
15 OR 20A, 120V BRANCH CIRCUITS					CITY	Tel. No.	
1 TO 10 INCLUSIVE EACH							
11 TO 40 INCLUSIVE EACH					PERMIT APPLICANT		
41 OR MORE BRANCH CIRCUITS EACH					ADDRESS		
15 OR 20A, 208V TO 277V LIGHTING EACH					CITY	Tel. No.	
RESIDENTIAL APPLIANCES UP TO 3HP Power Apparatus & Large Appliances					LICENSE OR REG. NUMBER		Class.
Size & Type HP, KW, KVA, or KVAR					DISTRICT NO.	PROCESSED BY	
_____ Up to 3 Incl.							
_____ Over 3 to 10 Incl.					FINAL DATE		
_____ Over 10 to 50 Incl.						VALIDATION	
_____ Over 50 to 100 Incl.					FINAL BY		
_____ Over 100							
Services, Swbd., MCC & Panelboards							
0 - 200 Amp. Under 600 V							
201 - 1000 Amp. Under 600 V							
Over 1000 Amp. or Over 600 V							
Temp. Power Pole & Appurtenances							
Sign with One Branch Circuit							
Additional Sign Branch Circuits							
Misc. Conduits & Conductors							
Other (See Complete Fee Schedule) _____				▶			
PERMIT FEE	(Sub-Total)						
PLAN CHECKING FEE							
PERMIT ISSUING FEE							
TOTAL FEE							

SEE REVERSE FOR EXPLANATORY LANGUAGE

Figure 2–2 (continued)

WORKER'S COMPENSATION DECLARATION

I hereby affirm that I have a certificate of consent to self insure, or a certificate of Worker's Compensation Insurance, or a certified copy thereof (Sec. 3800 Lab. C.)

Policy No. _____ Company _____

☐   Certified copy is hereby furnished.

☐   Certified copy is filed with the county building inspection department.

Date _____ Applicant _____

CERTIFICATE OF EXEMPTION FROM WORKERS' COMPENSATION INSURANCE

(This section need not be completed if the work involved by the permit is for one hundred dollars ($100) or less.)

I certify that in the performance of the work for which this permit is issued, I shall not employ any person in any manner so as to become subject to the Workers' Compensation Laws.

Date _____ Applicant _____

NOTICE TO APPLICANT: If, after making this Certificate of Exemption, you should become subject to the Workers' Compensation provisions of the Labor Code, you must forthwith comply with such provisions or this permit shall be deemed revoked.

LICENSED CONTRACTORS DECLARATION

I hereby affirm that I am licensed under provisions of Chapter 9 (commencing with Section 7000) of Division 3 of the Business and Professions Code, and my license is in full force and effect.

License Number _____ Lic. Class _____

Contractor _____ Date _____

☐   I am exempt under Sec. _____

B.&P.C. for this reason _____

_____ Date: _____

Signature _____

☐   Exemption for Reg. Maint. Elect.

SINGLE FAMILY
HOME OWNER-BUILDER DECLARATION

I hereby affirm that I am exempt from the Contractor's License Law for the following reason (Section 7031.5, Business and Professions Code):

☐   I, as owner of the property, will do the work and the structure is not intended or offered for sale (Section 7044, Business and Professions Code).

CONSTRUCTION LENDING AGENCY

I hereby affirm that there is a construction lending agency for the performance of the work for which this permit is issued (Sec. 3097, Civ. C.)

Lender's Name _____

Lender's Address _____

I certify that I have read this application and state that the above information is correct. I agree to comply with all County ordinances and State laws regulating Electrical wiring, and hereby authorize representatives of this County to enter upon the above-mentioned property for inspection purposes.

_____   _____
SIGNATURE OF APPLICANT OR AGENT   DATE

Figure 2–2 (continued)

APPROVALS	DATE	INSPECTOR'S SIGNATURE
TEMP POWER POLE		
UNDERSLAB WORK		
ROUGH CONDUIT		
WIRING		
FIXTURES		
POWER AUTHORIZED		
UTILITY CO. NOTIFIED		
FINAL	*Enter on Front*	

NOTES

Figure 2–2 (continued)

OWNER-BUILDER DECLARATION

I hereby affirm that I am exempt from the Contractor's License Law for the following reason *(Section 7031.5, Business and Professions Code): Any city or county which requires a permit to construct, alter, improve, demolish, or repair any structure, prior to its issuance, also requires the applicant for such permit to file a signed statement that he is licensed pursuant to the provisions of the Contractor's License Law (Chapter 9 (commencing with Section 7000) of Division 3 of the Business and Professions Code) or that he is exempt therefrom and the basis for the alleged exemption. Any violation of Section 7031.5 by any applicant for a permit subjects the applicant to a civil penalty of not more than five hundred dollars ($500):*

☐ I, as owner of the property will do the work, and the structure is not intended or offered for sale.
(Sec. 7044, Business and Professions Code: The Contractor's License Law does not apply to an owner of property who builds or improves thereon, and who does such work himself provided that such improvements are not intended or offered for sale. If, however, the building or improvement is sold within one year of completion, the owner-builder will have the burden of proving that he did not build or improve for the purpose of sale.)

I am exempt under Sec. _____

B & P.C. for this reason _____

_____

Date _____

Owner _____

and downspouts will be handled later on during the finish work but since the job may be performed by the same subcontractor, you can estimate for it now.

If your remodeling project involves any of these items, obtain estimates from sheet metal subcontractors and enter them on your estimate sheet under "Metal Work."

Roof

While I have known people who have taken on this task themselves, I generally do not recommend it. The danger of falling, of incurring a back injury, or of simply doing it incorrectly and having leakage is not worth the risk. Obtain your estimates from licensed roofing contractors and list the appropriate figure on your sheet under "Roof."

Windows

You may prefer the look of new wooden framed windows for your addition, but installing and maintaining them may not be worth the added cost. Many fine metal-framed windows on the market can be "dressed up" to resemble wood. By simply adding wood trim, these windows look great and are virtually maintenance free; you'll never need to paint them. They are very easy to remove and clean and, best of all, are generally less expensive than wood.

You may also wish to consider replacing your old existing wood windows with new metal framed replacement windows. Why pay to have those old windows scraped and painted every couple of years? These new, relatively inexpensive metal windows can be installed directly into your old wood window casings without the need for extensive patchwork. These windows are also nearly maintenance free and "pop out" for easy cleaning.

Contact your local building supply center and obtain estimates for the windows that are right for you. As always, find out if the supplier offers a contractor's discount and, if not, find one who does. If your supplier does not do installation, you will need to obtain a separate estimate for the labor to install the windows. Your rough framing or finish carpentry contractor can handle the job.

List these estimates under the "Mill Work" section of your Contractor's Estimate Sheet.

Doors

After choosing the style and type of doors that suit you, obtain estimates at your building material supplier. You may want your rough framing contractor to install the outside doors and your finish carpentry contractor to handle the interior ones. Since your rough framing contractor comes in first, having that person install the exterior doors would allow you to lock up the house sooner. Obtain estimates from both contractors.

The rough framer should build the frames for *all* doors and windows. Installation includes the doors themselves, all hinges, stops, casings, jambs, strike plates, and pass sets. Doors may also be purchased "prehung" in which case all your carpenter need do is install the complete door into a preset opening. Prehung doors can reduce installation labor costs, but they generally tend to be hollow and of lesser quality.

Enter your estimates for doors under "Mill Work."

Hardware (Finish)

All metal items that would be needed to install the windows and doors fall under this category. These include strike plates, pass sets (door knobs and latches), weather stripping, catches for cabinets and cupboards, sliding tracks for doors, knobs and handles, and any hardware items required for your project.

Estimate these items and enter their costs under "Hardware–Finish."

Insulation and Deadening

Here is another area where doing it yourself may accomplish some savings. Regardless of your local climate, you will probably need to install insulation in the remodeled area. To do this yourself, all you need is a good pair of gloves, a breathing mask, and a pair of safety glasses. The material you will need is not terribly expensive, and the installation is easy. Simply apply the fiberglass strips to the spaces between your studs. There is no need to nail the material because it is lightweight and will stay in place. Consult your plans to determine which insulation rating, or "R-value," is required for your particular job and obtain an estimate for material.

If you require some additional sound-absorbing or "deadening" board material, simply obtain material costs and an estimate from your finish carpenter for installation. Enter these estimates under "Miscellaneous" on your estimate sheet.

Exterior Wall Finish

Regardless of the type of exterior wall finish that you decide to use, you will need to obtain estimates. If you plan to have wood lap siding, you will need to talk with your finish carpenter for labor costs and your lumber-yard for the materials. Should your plans call for stucco, you will need to obtain cost estimates from stucco or exterior coating contractors. Brick siding will require estimates from a mason and a building material supplier.

Be sure to consider the possibility of needing to rent scaffolding for this phase and obtain an estimate. Your scaffolding supplier will deliver, set up, and dismantle upon completion for an all-inclusive price. Enter your scaffolding estimate under "Extras." Where most owner/builders go over budget is by not anticipating this kind of small detail. (The topic of going over budget is covered in greater detail later on in this chapter.)

Depending on the exterior siding you select, you will need to choose the appropriate category to enter your estimate. If you plan to stucco, enter your estimate under "Lath & Plastering–Exterior." Should you decide on wood lap siding, you would enter it under "Lumber–Finish" for material and under "Carpentry–Finish" for labor. If you have chosen brick, you would enter it under "Masonry–Face brick" section on your estimate sheet.

Interior Wall Finish

If your plans call for drywall (wallboard or Sheetrock, if you prefer those terms) or plaster, contact a contractor for an estimate for both the labor and materials. If possible, obtain separate prices for the labor and material and then obtain your own material estimates. Make sure that the contractor provides a complete list of the materials needed so that you can be sure you will be making a fair comparison. Since he will probably know your intent, he may be inclined to include his markup of the materials in his labor costs. This is why it is important to obtain three estimates. If you discover that these material costs are no higher than you can get yourself, you may just as well have the contractor order the materials.

Enter your estimate for drywall or plaster under "Lath & Plastering–Interior" on your estimate sheet.

Cabinets, Stair Work, and Other Wood Finish Work

Adding a kitchen or bathroom will almost certainly involve installing some type of cabinetry. Other items such as built-in bookshelves, closet organizers, and wet bars will require some mill work as well. You should decide whether you intend to order custom mill work for these items or to purchase some prefabricated pieces. Obtain your estimates accordingly.

If you add a second story and have stairs to install, you must consider the cost for the finish work. Remember that the rough framing of the stairs will be done during the beginning stages of your project. If your stairway is going to be framed by walls on either side and you plan on carpeting the steps, your only concern will be for adding a handrail. Your rough framer should have already done the rest. On the other hand, if you are planning a more traditional staircase, you will need to consider adding balusters, a handrail, end post(s), treads, stringers, and some molding. While most of these items can be purchased in prefabricated form, you will still require a skilled artisan to install them correctly. By having your draftsman estimate the correct number of steps (usually a minimum of 13 or 14), you can obtain costs for the materials. Your finish carpenter can then provide you with a cost for installation.

Although your finish carpenter can probably handle this work quite competently, you certainly don't want to risk paying him to get an education. Unless he is thoroughly skilled and knowledgeable in stair work, you may want to hire a stair specialist. A carpenter who is inexperienced with this specialized field could waste material or delay the completion of your project. If the carpenter you have decided to hire for the other finish work is comfortable with staircases, he will tell you. Ask him how many he has done in his career and if you can see some of his work.

List your estimates for these items under "Mill Work" on the Contractor's Estimate Sheet.

Tile Work

If you have planned for tiling in the bathrooms or kitchen, you will need estimates for both labor and materials. You may not yet know which type and style of ceramic tile you will use, so you may have to do some guessing on the material costs. Visit your wholesale tile distributor and determine some general price ranges. To protect yourself here, choose the most expensive tile that you think you might consider and base your estimate on that number. Ask the tile contractors to estimate not only their labor costs but also the approximate square footage of the material they will need. Then list these costs under "Tile" on your estimate sheet.

Floors

This phase of your project is probably one of the easiest to estimate. By now, you should have a pretty clear idea of the type of flooring you plan to use. Wall-to-wall carpeting, hardwood (strip or tongue and groove, parquet, and plank), ceramic tile, and vinyl (sheet or tiles) are the major available options.

If you choose carpeting, you will need to obtain estimates for padding, installation, and the carpet itself. Some carpet stores offer a package price for all three, but generally you should avoid this arrangement unless you have a choice of padding in such a package. Padding is very important and too often is overlooked.

I recommend that you find a wholesale carpet padding distributor and obtain a price on 5-pound density "rebond." This type of padding looks like (and is) scraps of multicolored foam recycled by being bonded together. Some people try to save money by selecting inexpensive padding such as plain foam. Others pay more for felt padding. This is a big mistake, especially for your own home. Felt padding is very firm and durable, which is okay for commercial buildings, but it makes a poor choice for residential use. Both felt and plain foam padding offer very little cushioning for your feet. Rebond, on the other hand, is not that much more expensive than plain foam (particularly if you purchase it wholesale), and it will extend the life of your carpet. It also will provide greater comfort for your feet. By all means, avoid "waffle" padding, which is made of clay, among other things, and tends to deteriorate into dust under normal wear and tear.

For the carpet itself, you again should try to deal directly with the mill or a wholesale distributor. For estimating purposes, again figure on the high side. This will give you some latitude if you have not yet selected the exact carpet you intend to install. Prices for both labor and materials are provided on a per-square-yard basis.

If you have selected wood for your flooring, you should get a labor price from a contractor who specializes in installing hardwood floors. As with the staircase, this can be specialized work and you will want the best skilled professional for the job.

For installing linoleum, you will again want to hire an expert to avoid waste and assure a good job. Some people have saved by installing the vinyl themselves, but I would recommend this only if you really know what you are doing. If you should decide to do it yourself without the benefit of the experience, you could wipe out any savings you might have had by wasting your material. The same is true for installing wallpaper. Unless you really feel confident about what you are doing, leave it to a professional.

Enter your estimates for flooring under the "Floors" section of your estimate sheet.

Carpentry (Finish)

This phase would involve such elements as the installation of interior doors, moldings, wood fireplace mantels, cabinetry installation, wood closet organizers, and any other finish carpentry work required under your particular project. Have your finish carpenter provide labor costs and estimate the material you will need. Enter your estimates under "Carpentry–Finish" on your estimate sheet.

Electrical (Finish)

As with the rough electrical work discussed earlier, you have an excellent opportunity for some substantial savings here. Anyone can quickly learn how to install plugs, light switches, and fixtures. Simply have your electrician make all connections to the panel and leave the breaker switches in the off position. Then install the necessary items on your own time.

You can also experience savings by shopping for the fixtures and other hardware needed to complete the electrical phase of the project yourself. To obtain your material list, you need only count the number of switches and plug outlets along with any overhead fixtures and electric smoke detectors required directly from your plans. Then obtain estimates for this material. Just be sure to remember to obtain an estimate from your electrician for his part in the finish work. Enter these estimates under "Electrical."

Plumbing (Finish)

You will need an estimate from your plumber for labor costs to install your plumbing fixtures. You can purchase all toilets, sinks, faucets, showers, and bathtubs using the discounting methods we will discuss throughout this book. It is best to stick to neutral colors, such as white and beige, when you select fixtures to avoid having a potential buyer turned off by the prospect of having to replace them when you try to sell your home. Black, forest green, or mauve may look great to you, but others may not share your tastes (see also Chapter 1).

Create a category for finish plumbing under "Sanitation" and list your costs there.

Shower Doors and Mirrors

In some instances, installation of shower doors and mirrors can actually be completed after you've finished painting and wallpapering. After talking with your subcontractors, you will know which schedule works best for you.

For this phase of your project, installation is customarily included in the purchase of your materials. As with the other materials, always deal with suppliers who offer you a contractor's discount and obtain at least three different bids. This can usually be done over the phone simply by measuring the area yourself and telling them what you want. If it is practical for you to do so, deal directly with the manufacturer on a wholesale basis (see Chapter 5 and Appendix C).

Enter your estimates for these items under "Glazing" on the Contractor's Estimate Sheet.

Concrete (Finish)

If your plans include repairing or installing a concrete driveway, steps, walkways, and/or curbs, obtain estimates for this work. Even if you only plan to repair or install an asphalt driveway, enter your estimates under the "Concrete" section of your estimate sheet.

If your plans call for brick steps, walkways, or driveway, you may enter your estimates under "Masonry."

Cleanup

We have already talked about the necessity of a trash bin for the cleanup phase of your project. You will have budgeted for this in the "Miscellaneous–Removing Debris" section. In addition to the bin, however, some labor will be required for the final cleanup phase. It will be your responsibility to organize this effort and estimate the costs involved.

Since at this point you cannot accurately estimate how much cleanup will be necessary, you are really going to have to take a guess here. After you have made your guess, you had better double it for estimating purposes. For example, if you think that it may take two laborers three full days to clean everything up and to load the trash bin, estimate that it will take six days instead.

For the cleanup–labor category, create a new heading under the "Miscellaneous" section or, if you prefer, in the "Extras" section of the estimate sheet.

Estimates are also necessary for the cleaning of any new windows. From the time they are installed until your project is completed, these windows will get very dirty. You can obtain an estimate from a professional window cleaner and enter those costs on your estimate sheet. Here again, you may choose to clean the windows yourself but at least you have budgeted for the option. Enter this estimate under "Miscellaneous–Cleaning Windows."

Landscaping

Many people tend to overlook this area. If you are expanding the footprint of your home or even if you are not, there will be some disruption of your landscape. You should consider the costs for adding or replacing grass, shrubbery, trees, and possibly even an automatic watering system. Enter estimates for these items under "Landscaping" on your estimate sheet.

INCLUDING THE COST OF PAINTING AND DECORATING IN YOUR ESTIMATE

I have included these items with their own subheading because they are frequently overlooked in estimating costs. As a result, this part of the project often doesn't get finished until long after completion of the actual construction phase. Many people simply run out of money because they failed to include these items in their original budget.

Surely you have been to people's homes months after they have undergone remodeling and heard them say: "Oh. . . . As you can see, we are still in the process of decorating." In most cases, this is because they never gave any thought to completing the decoration phase once it was finally built. By doing some advanced planning, you can prevent this from happening to you.

You may want to wait until after you've "lived" with the new addition for a while before you plan the decorating. This is fine but you can still estimate for such labor items as hanging wallpaper and painting.

Determining how much paint you will need is easy. Just consult your plans and estimate the total square footage of the wall and ceiling space requiring paint and/or a sealant (for wallpaper). You can also decide whether to do the painting yourself or to hire someone to do the work. Obviously, you can experience some savings here if you do it yourself. To be safe, however, obtain three bids from painting contractors for estimating purposes.

It is also possible to estimate for the cost for wallpaper itself. Have your paperhanger estimate the amount of material you might need, then shop for the most expensive paper you think you might use and obtain costs. Your paperhanger will also give you a "per roll" cost for the labor to do the work. To estimate labor costs, simply multiply the number of rolls estimated by the per roll cost given.

Remember, at this point you are just "estimating" costs to ensure that you will have enough money to complete your project. Chapter 5 explains how you can cut costs when it actually comes time to buy the materials you will need. Therefore, don't hesitate to estimate on the high side at this stage.

You can use another method to estimate this important phase in very general terms. Some professionals have suggested that you can expect to pay about 10% of the total cost of all other items on your estimate projections for painting and decorating. This means that you could expect to pay as much as $4,000 extra on a $40,000 remodeling project. You may not actually need this much but it doesn't hurt to cover yourself.

Enter your estimates for "Painting & Decorating" on your estimate sheet.

Should You Plan to Use a Professional Decorator?

This area is strictly a matter of personal taste, your budget constraints, and the extent to which decorating will be necessary. Some people are very talented at interior decoration. If you have the ability and the time to plan and decorate the improved area yourself, you will certainly save money. Some homeowners, though, find it much more effective to call in a professional decorator. To them, the benefits far outweigh the costs.

In one project, I decided to extend a bathroom's tile from the floor to a height of 4 feet around the room. It was an important consideration at that point because the drywall in the rest of the addition was being applied lengthwise in two strips. Each sheet of drywall is 4 feet wide, and in this case it was 12 feet in length (see Chapter 4). The two pieces resting atop one another equaled the ceiling height of 8 feet. If we followed through with my idea, we would only need one "strip" (four feet) around the top half of the room since there would be lath, cement, and tile around the lower half.

After checking with some local realtors and friends for several referrals, we decided to hire a terrific decorator recognized as a member of the American Society of Interior Designers (ASID). Membership in this professional organization requires graduation from four- or five-year degree programs along with very stringent testing procedures and at least two years' experience. Designers who have yet to achieve a passing grade on the test but who are otherwise eligible are considered "Allied Members." If you would like a list of at least three ASID members in your area, consult the white pages of your telephone book or call information for the office of the ASID chapter nearest you. The national offices for ASID are listed in Appendix A.

Because we brought the decorator into the project before the completion stages, the results were far more spectacular and economical than if we had done it on our own. She quickly convinced me that installing tile to 4-foot height in the bathroom would make it more closely resemble a gym locker room than an elegant master bathroom.

In this case, the professional's decorating services were well worth the additional cost. In fact, a really good decorator can actually increase the value of your home along with making it easier to sell. Perhaps more important, he or she can help you avoid costly decorating or design errors that may be expensive to replace later on.

Interior decorators generally work their fees in one of two ways. Either they will take a markup on the cost of the materials you buy through them or they will bill you on an hourly basis for consultation. These hourly fees can range anywhere from $25 for an unaccredited decorator to as high as $100 or more per hour for an ASID professional. Decorators who prefer to use the markup method will generally mark up the materials they purchase wholesale as much as 30% to 50%.

I recommend the hourly consultation method because you can maintain better control over the cost of your materials. If you choose this method and your decorator should allow you to purchase at cost and directly from wholesale suppliers, this will be even better for you. Although it may not be any less expensive this way, at least you can more accurately calculate the cost of the decorator's time. Separating the labor costs from the material costs allows you to see just where you are spending your money.

If you do choose the hourly consultation method, ask the interior designer to estimate how long it will take to complete the job. Better yet, develop a budget for time that you think you can live with and ask the decorator if it seems sufficient to do a first-class job. Enter this estimate under "Painting & Decorating–Special Decorating."

The decision to bring in a decorator is entirely up to you. However, if you even think that you may consider it, at least estimate for it. By doing so, you ensure that you will not be short of the funds later on. If you do decide to hire a decorator, you would be well advised to have a consultation prior to ordering or purchasing your tile, bathroom fixtures, and carpeting.

A SECOND BUDGET FOR FURNISHINGS

When you have completed your remodeling project you will probably have some area added to your home. Have you given any thought to what you plan to put in the newly added space? Obviously, this is not going to be a serious concern if you have expanded your kitchen or added a bathroom since you will have probably already given some thought to your appliances and fixtures for these rooms. But what about a bedroom, family room, den, or recreation room? Do you already own furniture that will outfit and compliment your new addition? If the answer is no, you had better give some thought to the furniture you will need.

Although it is not necessary to add the costs for these items to your Contractor's Estimate Sheet, it is a good idea to develop a second estimate sheet for furnishings and to include the costs for your decorator if you choose to hire one. By planning ahead, you will avoid having to delay the purchasing of your furnishings simply because you run out of money.

THE BUDGET KILLERS

You may recall from Chapter 1 that the average remodeling runs at least 20% over budget. In fact, this is our sixth rule for successful remodeling. How can we go over budget when we have been so careful to obtain accurate estimates? In a word: *extras.*

This word, perhaps more than any other term that you are going to hear during the course of your project, will cause the hair on the back of your head to rise and send shivers up your spine. It may come to you in this way: You will be discussing something with your subcontractor, who will say, "Oh. . . . Well, that will be extra." To which, you will ask something like this: "Well, just how much 'extra' are we talking about here?" The response will be, "Gee, I don't know . . . we will have to just see when we get into it."

In Chapter 4, we will consider ways to deal with this problem. You will learn the importance of requiring written authorization and an agreed-upon price prior to the contractor's beginning any additional work. Just understand, at this point, that no matter how carefully you plan and estimate your project, it is inevitable that either you will overlook something or something additional will reveal itself once you have started the job. You may also change your mind or alter details of your planned project after you are underway. These changes, whether intentional or unintentional, will most assuredly cause you to go over budget.

So how do you account for going over budget in your original estimates? To some degree, you already have. By estimating on the high side and by using the subcontractors' estimates for nearly all phases of the project instead of counting on the savings created by doing work yourself, you have effectively built in a 20% cushion. If you choose to do none of the work yourself, it would be helpful for you to understand in which areas you are more likely to go over budget and why.

Your initial phases—Architectural, Preliminary, Legal, Excavating, Concrete–Rough, Masonry–Rough, Lumber–Rough, Carpentry–Rough, Sanitation–Plumbing, Sanitation–Sewer, Metal Work, Roof, Lath & Plastering–Exterior, Hardware–Rough, Heating, and Insurance—are all areas where you should fall well within budget. These items are generally fixed expenses. Unless you alter your plans substantially, the numbers should not change much. You are more likely to go over budget in the areas following these phases.

The finish work—Concrete–Finish, Masonry–Finish, Lumber–Finish, Carpentry–Finish, Sanitation–Finish (Plumbing Fixtures), Lath & Plastering–Interior, Hardware–Finish, Electrical, Mill Work, Glazing, Tile, Painting & Decorating, Floors, Miscellaneous items, and Extras—have great potential for going over budget. Why? Because you are more likely to make changes, errors, and upgrades in some or all of these areas.

For example, let us assume that your project is now well underway. You decide that you want the electrician to add recessed lighting rather than the single overhead light in the original plans. Just last week you visited a home with this type of lighting, and you decided that you would like the same for your home.

You discuss this with your electrician and agree that it will be "'extra," but you concur that the change will be most dramatic and well worth the additional cost. Your electrician gives you a price for the additional labor, and then you obtain the additional material costs for the lights themselves. The problem will be, however, that the electrician will need to break out some plaster to accommodate the additional wiring. This means that you are also going to require a price for additional patchwork from your plastering subcontractor. This is a prime example of how a change in one decision can affect the cost in another area.

If you are not planning to do any work yourself and have made no allowances for going over budget, you should add 20% to the finish areas outlined above. By doing so, you will protect yourself from inevitable changes. If it turns out that you don't need all the money you may have borrowed for the project, you can always apply it back toward the principal payment of the loan (see Chapter 3). It is far better to have budgeted for more money than you will need rather than the reverse.

Keep in mind that a budget is an "approximation" of what you plan to spend. Where you eventually wind up in relation to your original budget may depend on just how well you have managed the entire project. If you have done your job effectively using the suggested methods and guidelines presented here, you should end up with a better job for less money.

REVIEW

- Carefully assemble your costs and list them on an estimate sheet.

- Consider those areas where you may be able to save money by doing it yourself or by utilizing your own labor force.

- Use contractor's costs for estimating purposes even if you plan to do the work yourself. This will give you a cushion for other areas where you may go over budget.

- Review and understand the order in which the various phases of your project will take place.

- Hire "specialists" to avoid cost overruns from material waste.

- Consider the advantages of installing maintenance free metal-framed windows and metal-framed replacement windows.

- If you choose to have carpeting installed, consider rebond padding.

- Remember to estimate for painting and decorating.

- Consider hiring a professional decorator and if you do, remember to arrange for a consultation before ordering tile, fixtures, and carpeting.

- Select the hourly consultation method with a decorator, if practical, to separate labor from material costs.

- Create a second budget for furnishings.

- Understand the areas in which you are likely to go over budget and plan accordingly.

Where and How to Obtain the Money for Your Remodeling Project

Regardless of the remodeling project you have in mind, you clearly will need to spend some money. What may not yet be so clear is where you will get the money. This chapter covers the subject of financing in depth and provides some helpful suggestions. I will assume that you do not plan to use your life savings (cash) to complete this project. Even if you do plan to use your own cash, you should at least review this chapter to determine if there is a better alternative.

These suggestions will not perfectly suit every individual. I would strongly urge you to discuss these ideas with your accountant or other financial advisor to determine the best course of action for your particular situation.

REFINANCE YOUR FIRST MORTGAGE

At the time this book is being written, we are experiencing the most favorable mortgage home loan interest rates in the past 14 years. If you took out a home mortgage loan in the late 1970s or early 1980s, you may have paid as much as 20% (or more) on the money you borrowed. Today, you may find rates as low as 8.5% for a 30-year fixed rate mortgage loan. Thus, it may be an ideal time for you to refinance your home for the purpose of funding your remodeling project.

As an example, let us assume that you purchased your home in August 1983 for $170,000. At that time, you obtained a first mortgage loan of 80% of the purchase price, or $136,000, and the interest rate on your loan was 14.5% fixed for 30 years. Your payments would be about $1,665.40 per month, including principal and interest, for 360 months (30 years). Of course, you paid some loan origination fees of approximately 2% of the loan amount or $2,720 but let's not be concerned about that at this point. For simplicity, we'll also assume that there is no other financing on your home.

As of August 1991 the property's value has increased to approximately $275,000. You now want to remodel your home, and your estimates tell you the work will cost just under $40,000. It is hard to believe but you have paid more than $159,800 in mostly interest and very little principal during the past eight years. If you were to refinance and pay off your old loan now, you would still owe more than $132,000. Remember though, if you refinance at a lower interest rate you will pay less interest on that same $132,000. Check to see if your original loan permits the bank to assess a "prepayment penalty" that may make refinancing a less appealing option.

Once you have decided to refinance, you should think about borrowing enough not only to cover your remodeling costs but also to pay the "up front" fees charged for loaning you the money. Most lending institutions will charge you "points" (loan fees) to write a new first mortgage loan. The fees charged will vary depending on the lender and are sometimes negotiable. Don't hesitate to ask for lower fees.

With more traditional lenders such as banks or savings and loans, you may be able to obtain lower fees if you bring your banking business to them. Many banks will also offer a reduced interest rate if you authorize them to withdraw loan payments directly from your account. Some lenders may even allow you to trade a slightly higher percentage rate for reduced up-front fees. Before choosing this path, compute the numbers both ways to determine which method works out better for you in the long run. If you are not sure just how to do the computations, review the arrangement with your accountant or financial advisor. He will be able to provide you with the tax considerations as well.

Getting back to our exercise, we will assume that the loan fees will be 2 points or 2% of the amount borrowed. Because we already know that we need $132,000 to pay off the existing first mortgage and another $40,000 to do the improvements, we are going to borrow at least $176,000 ($176,000 × 2% = $3,520 in loan fees) ($176,000 – $132,000 – $3,520 = $40,480 for the project).

Since most lenders will probably not loan more than 75% of the home's appraised value on a refinance and this house can be appraised for $275,000, we fall well within their lending guidelines. The loan-to-value ratio (LTV) in this particular case would be 64% (176,000 ÷ 275,000 = .64 or 64%). The amortized monthly payment on $176,000 at 9.5% fixed interest would be about $1,480 for 30 years. Note that we are dealing solely with fixed interest mortgage rates. While variable rate loans can have some advantages, it is impossible to compute the ultimate amount of interest to be paid.

What conclusions can we draw from the preceding refinancing exercise? Well, first of all, we have used the equity in our home to acquire the funds needed to complete our remodeling project. We have also reduced our monthly loan payments by about $185.40 per month ($1,665.40 on the old loan – $1,480 on the new one = $185.40 in monthly savings). Furthermore, we have reduced the amount of interest we were paying on the original loan from 14.5% down to 9.5%.

You may already have taken advantage of lower rates, and refinanced at about 11% interest. To determine if it will benefit you to refinance again down to 9.5%, you really have to compute carefully and compare the numbers for each option.

Because of the loan fees involved, it is not as simple as just selecting the lower interest rate. You have to figure out how much lower the new interest rate needs to be before it becomes worth the added fees. To do this you need to know how long it will take you to recoup the fees through your reduced payments. You can compute this by dividing the loan fees you will have to pay by the savings you will experience each month from reduced interest payments. This will tell you how many months it will take you before you realize any real savings.

Using the numbers discussed before, let us assume that you still owe $132,000 on your existing first mortgage, but in August 1988 you did refinance that loan and your current fixed interest rate is 11%. Your amortized monthly payment is now about $1,257 for 30 years. At this point, we will not concern ourselves with the additional $40,000 that we will need for our project since the need for that money is a given. For now, we just want to know if we should refinance the existing first mortgage along with it.

We are told that the fees amount to 2% of the borrowed funds for a 9.5% fixed rate mortgage. Our fees on the first $132,000 will be $2,640 (132,000 × 2% = $2640). The monthly payment on our new 30-year amortized 9.5% loan will be about $1,110. The difference between the old monthly payments and the new will be about $147 (1,257 − 1,110 = $147). Following our formula, we compute that it will take almost a year and a half before we begin to realize a savings from the reduced interest rate ($2,640 in fees ÷ $147 in monthly savings = approximately 18 months). If you plan to live in your home for more than 18 months, it may be worth it for you to refinance to the lower rate. Here again, I recommend that you consult with your accountant or other financial consultant to determine the right answers for you.

To assist you in your own analysis by computing amortized monthly payments on a mortgage that you are considering, see Figure 3–1.

ADD A SECOND MORTGAGE

It you have already refinanced your existing first mortgage to obtain a lower interest rate or your terms were favorable to begin with, you may want to consider a second mortgage. Although the interest rates on second mortgages are generally higher than first mortgages, the bank fees are minimal or nonexistent. Currently, some very favorable secondary financing options are available.

As we have already established, most banks and other mortgage lenders will loan up to 75% of a home's value for whatever reason you choose. Providing, of course, that you have sufficient income to repay the loan. Later in this chapter, I will discuss in greater detail what lenders will expect from you. At this point, we will assume that you have sufficient income and an excellent credit history and that this option is available to you.

Adding a second mortgage to your existing home financing has advantages and disadvantages. Competition among mortgage lenders is

Figure 3–1

Amortized Monthly Mortgage Payments

To compute *approximate* amortized monthly mortgage payments using this table, simply multiply the amount of your anticipated loan in 1000s by the factor that corresponds to the correct interest amount. For example, if your loan amount is $125,250 and the interest rate is 9.75% for 30 years you would multiply 125.25 × 8.59 = approximately $1,076.

Interest Rate	30 Years per $1000	15 Years per $1000
8.50	7.69	9.85
8.75	7.87	9.99
9.00	8.05	10.14
9.25	8.23	10.29
9.50	8.41	10.44
9.75	8.59	10.59
10.00	8.78	10.75
10.25	8.96	10.90
10.50	9.15	11.05
10.75	9.33	11.21
11.00	9.52	11.37
11.25	9.71	11.52
11.50	9.90	11.68
11.75	10.09	11.84
12.00	10.29	12.00
12.25	10.48	12.16
12.50	10.67	12.33

fierce for this type of business and one may offer a better deal than the next. Some banks may charge absolutely no fees at all, and others may ask from $300 to $500 for what some institutions call "appraisal" or "documentation" fees. If you shop around, these low or no fee loans are clearly advantageous.

Another advantage in obtaining a second mortgage is that you may borrow the money, receive it all at once, and use it for whatever purpose you wish. If your project is only going to cost you $40,000 to complete but you want to borrow another $10,000 for furnishings and to pay off some credit cards, this is perfectly okay. Lenders don't really care what you use the money for as long as you make your payments and their position is protected by sufficient value in the home (the 75% loan-to-value rule). Just remember that borrowing money is an expense. I do not recommend that you borrow a lot more money than you need because ultimately you will have to repay it, with interest.

One disadvantage would be that these types of loans generally charge higher interest rates than primary financing. You can expect to pay as much as 2 percentage points or more above rates for a first mortgage. Fixed rates of 11.25% to 12% are common in today's market. Another disadvantage is that repayment of fixed rate second mortgages is generally spread over a shorter time with terms usually extending from 5 to 15 years. While this will increase your monthly payment, your equity will build up faster and you will ultimately pay less interest over the life of the loan. The example used earlier in this chapter will illustrate my point.

We already determined that if you purchased a home in 1983 for $170,000 and obtained financing of $136,000, your amortized monthly payment on the 30-year fixed mortgage at 14.5% interest would be $1,665.40. If the terms of your loan had been for 15 years rather than 30 years, your payment would have been $1,857.08 monthly. You would have paid a total of $191.68 more per month than under the terms of the 30-year loan. That's just over $2,300 per year. It is now 1991 and you want to pay off that existing first mortgage. You have paid approximately $18,400 more over the past eight years ($2,300 × 8 = $18,400). What amount would now pay off that old first mortgage? $97,652 is the balance owing after eight years. Subtracting this figure from the payoff under the terms of the 30-year note gives a total of $34,348 ($132,000 − $97,652 = $34,348). Now we take the additional amount we paid in for the shorter mortgage and subtract it from this number and we are left with $15,948 in savings

($34,348 − $18,400 = $15,948). We are, of course, ignoring any tax advantages on the mortgage interest deduction but the message is clear. *If you can make a slightly greater monthly payment, select a shorter payoff period for huge savings.*

CONSIDER A HOME EQUITY LINE OF CREDIT

A number of home equity line of credit products are available from different lenders, but the essentials are similar. The lender will record a second trust deed against your property to the full amount of your credit line. The amount offered will depend on the equity you have in your home and your ability to support the loan payments, as determined by your income.

Using our previous example, let us assume that you decide not to refinance your first mortgage and that you still owe $132,000. We have established that your home can be appraised at $275,000. If your income is sufficient to support the maximum line and the lender is willing to loan up to 75% LTV, your home equity line would be $74,250 (275,000 × 75% = 206,250 − 132,000 = 74,250).

Under this program, you do not actually receive, or draw, the money until you physically need it. In this way, you do not begin paying interest on the borrowed money until you use it. You can draw out the money by either writing checks or by using a special credit card issued against your credit line account. This may be a real advantage to you because it will generally take time before you actually begin to draw on the money. Also, because you pay your various subcontractors over a period spanning the entire length of the project, you will only need large amounts of money at staggered intervals.

The rates for this type of loan product are based on a spread or margin above the current U.S. prime rate. This rate is known as an index, and your loan rate will generally be from one to three points above it. The interest rate that you are charged will vary over the life of the loan and will fluctuate with the index from which it is determined. If, for example, the prime rate is currently 8.5%, you could expect to pay interest of 10.5% if your loan's spread is 2 percentage points above the index. Your interest rate could vary with the index as often as every

30 days. If the prime rate were to jump to 9% after 30 days, the interest you would be paying on the outstanding balance would also adjust to 11% if the spread is 2%.

With some lenders, your interest and principal payments would not be amortized for the first 5 to 10 years, during what is known as the drawing period. You would simply pay interest only on the borrowed amount. After the drawing period ends, your loan would then be amortized over the life of the repayment period to include principal and interest payments. You always have the option of repaying the outstanding balance plus all interest due at any time during either the drawing period or the repayment period. As with other types of home mortgages, the interest on this type of loan is deductible to you on your taxes if you meet certain criteria. I will discuss these criteria later in this chapter.

The fees to process this type of loan will vary depending on the lender. Here again, however, competition among lenders favors the borrower. Some lenders will charge as little as $400 for "documentation fees" plus a nominal annual fee of around $35. You may pay a slightly higher interest rate for these low fees, but it may present a better alternative to paying substantially higher loan origination fees in return for obtaining a lower spread.

USE A HOME IMPROVEMENT LOAN FOR MINOR PROJECTS

If the improvements you wish to make are relatively minor (under $25,000) you may consider a home improvement loan. These loans are similar to other secondary financing products with a few exceptions. Although such loans are recorded against the title of your property, they are generally approved very quickly; you can have your money in as little as two weeks. Your lender will need only to verify your good credit and assess that you have sufficient equity in your home. It is generally not necessary for them to do a full-blown appraisal and title search. They will, however, wish to review your improvement plans and may stipulate that you use the money only for those specific improvements.

These loans generally have a shorter repayment period (5 to 10 years). Your interest rate will be the same as that offered for the other types of secondary financing previously discussed. However, the shorter payback period will make your monthly payments higher. If you can

Figure 3–2

Amortized Monthly Payment Schedule

To compute *approximate* amortized monthly mortgage payments using this table, simply multiply the amount of your anticipated loan in 1000s by the factor that corresponds to the correct interest amount. For example, if your loan amount is $25,000 and the interest rate is 11.50% for 10 years, you would multiply 25 × 14.06 = approximately $351.50.

Interest Rate	15 Years per $1000	10 Years per $1000	5 Years per $1000
9.50	10.44	12.94	21.00
9.75	10.59	13.08	21.12
10.00	10.75	13.22	21.25
10.25	10.90	13.35	21.37
10.50	11.05	13.49	21.49
10.75	11.21	13.63	21.62
11.00	11.37	13.77	21.74
11.25	11.52	13.92	21.87
11.50	11.68	14.06	21.99
11.75	11.84	14.20	22.12
12.00	12.00	14.35	22.24
12.25	12.16	14.49	22.37
12.50	12.33	14.64	22.50
12.75	12.49	14.78	22.63
13.00	12.65	14.93	22.75
13.25	12.82	15.08	22.88
13.50	12.98	15.23	23.01

afford the payments, this becomes an advantage because of the long-term savings. It may be considered a disadvantage if the higher monthly payout puts you in a financial pinch.

Figure 3–2 will assist you in your own analysis by showing amortized monthly payments on second mortgages, home equity lines of credit, and home improvement loans.

TAKE OUT A TITLE I FHA HOME IMPROVEMENT LOAN ONLY IF YOU HAVE LITTLE OR NO EQUITY

If you are unable to qualify for these other types of loans because you have very little or no equity built up in your home, you may consider a Title I home improvement loan offered with the backing of the federal government. The Federal Housing Administration (FHA) will guarantee a home improvement loan of up to $17,500 under certain conditions and restrictions. The loans themselves, though backed by the government, will be written and supervised by banks and other FHA-approved lending institutions. These loans can be processed in as little as 2 to 3 weeks, but there are disadvantages.

To qualify for this type of loan, you must have an excellent credit history and the money can only be used for specific home improvements. You must restrict your improvements to nonluxury projects. Building a koi pond or an outdoor spa would not qualify. You must use the money for acceptable remodeling projects such as building a room addition or a bathroom, or improving your kitchen.

When applying for the loan, you will find it necessary to provide a detailed outline of your home improvement project. The bank or other lending institution will be responsible for verifying that you complete the promised work. Normally, the improvements must be finished within a 6-month period. If, for valid reasons, the work is not completed during this time, the lender can extend the completion deadline for up to another 6 months. If the work is still incomplete at that time, the lender can foreclose on the loan, which is a major drawback to this type of financing.

Another disadvantage is that the bank or other lending institution can charge a ridiculously high amount in fees for the loan. Fees ranging from 5% to 10% of the loan amount are not at all uncommon. Most banks are reluctant to deal with these loans because of the time needed to ensure compliance. As a result, institutions who offer these loans can be hard to find. If you need help in locating an FHA Title I lending institution in your area call the government agency at (800) 733-4663.

My advice on obtaining at least three estimates from all suppliers applies here as well. Mortgage and other money lenders are no different from any other supplier you will deal with during your project. You should analyze the estimates you obtain and select the rate and terms that work best for you.

THE TAX ADVANTAGES OF THE HOME MORTGAGE INTEREST DEDUCTION

All the various mortgage loans we have discussed up to this point offer certain favorable tax considerations. It would be worthwhile to review some of these advantages before we go on to alternative financing methods that may not share these same tax benefits.

The Internal Revenue Service (IRS) publishes a very useful guide on home mortgage interest deductions. The guide, called *Publication 936,* is available from your local IRS office or from your accountant. According to this publication, you may, in most cases, deduct all your home mortgage interest expenses providing you meet certain criteria: "This (mortgage interest deduction) applies to any loans secured by your main home, including first and second mortgages, home equity loans and refinanced mortgages." It goes on to state that you can deduct your interest expenses on the following home loans:

- Mortgages you took out on or before October 13, 1987 (called grandfather debt).

- Mortgages you took out after October 13, 1987, to buy, build, or improve your home (called home acquisition debt), but only if these mortgages plus any grandfathered debt totaled $1 million or less throughout (1991).

- Mortgages you took out after October 13, 1987, other than to buy, build, or improve your home (called home equity debt), but only if these mortgages totaled $100,000 or less throughout (1991).

You also need to be aware of the following factors:

- If you are married and file a separate return, the home acquisition debt limit is $500,000 and the home equity debt limit is $50,000.

- If you had a main home and a second home, the home acquisition and home equity debt dollar limits apply to the total mortgages on both homes.

Make sure you have the most current information and familiarize yourself thoroughly with IRS *Publication 936* and other related IRS publications, and discuss these deductions with your accountant. Some other factors may apply in your particular case. For most of us, however, the rules are fairly clear: if you have not exceeded the $1 million dollar limit and *all* your loan proceeds are used for your home improvements, the interest is deductible on your taxes in the year in which they were paid.

There are also some special rules with respect to deducting the amount you paid in "points" or loan fees on the money you borrowed. Here again, consult with your accountant or the IRS for accurate information.

It is extremely important for you to keep every receipt that you obtain during your remodeling project as it will be your responsibility to prove that the money you borrowed was actually spent on your project. If your tax returns are ever audited, you will need these receipts to substantiate your claims.

Once your project gets underway, you will not believe the number of receipts you will acquire, particularly if you buy many of the materials yourself. Even if you plan to pay for everything with checks, I can assure you that there will be times where you will run out for some small items and wind up using cash. Also, checks will not prove what the money was used for. I recommend that you get a large, expandable, and closable folder from your local stationery store for this purpose. It is important to keep receipts even if you don't use a loan secured by your home. If you ever plan to sell your home, or even if you die while you still own it, you or your heirs will need them to determine your home's cost basis. The IRS will not be interested in what you *think* you spent.

WHAT BANKS OR OTHER MORTGAGE LENDERS LOOK FOR

Once you have decided either to refinance your home or to apply secondary financing to obtain the required funds, you need to learn the lending institution's criteria for approving loans to determine your chances of approval. This information may help you to take steps that will ensure your success.

All lenders will concentrate their attention primarily on three things. The first is the status of your credit. Each lender to whom you apply for a loan will obtain and review the latest credit report available on you. All lenders subscribe to a credit reporting agency and need only your social security number to access your current credit file. This written report will contain any or all of the following pertinent information that may apply to you:

- All types of loans and other credit extended to you including loans secured by real estate or other valuable consideration, unsecured personal loans, major credit cards, and revolving store credit.

- Your record on payment for all past and current loans including slow payments, bad debt writeoffs due to nonpayment, timely payment, any penalties charged for late payment, loan defaults, and foreclosures.

- Whether you had any collections, judgments, liens, repossessions, creditor lawsuits, wage attachments, or garnishments of wages.

Most lenders will view most unfavorably any major negative items listed in your report such as a bankruptcy, loan default, foreclosure, repossession, judgment, wage attachment or garnishment, creditor lawsuit, property lien, bad debt writeoff, or slow payment record. All bankruptcy information will remain in your credit file for 10 years. Other negative information will be removed after 7 years. Be aware that while favorable credit information on current accounts will remain on your report indefinitely, it will be far overshadowed by any negative information.

You have to keep in mind that lenders do not really like having to foreclose on real property regardless of how much they are protected by a loan-to-value ratio. These lenders are in the business of making good loans, not turning a profit by selling foreclosed real estate. They simply do not want to carry bad loans on their books or to undergo the legal hassles involved with the foreclosure process. Your past credit history, while not necessarily indicative of future events, at least provides lenders with some measure of your credit management responsibility.

If you have not done so recently, it would be a very good idea for you to request a copy of your current credit profile. You are ultimately responsible for seeing to it that the information in your credit report is correct and current. You may be required to pay a small fee for this information unless you have recently been denied credit based on the data in your file. If that is the case, you need only request a copy of your credit report and one will be provided to you free of charge. To obtain a copy of your current credit profile or to correct any inaccuracies that may exist in your file, contact the most widely used consumer credit reporting agency in your area by referring to Appendix B. It may even be a good idea for you to obtain a copy of your credit profile from all three major agencies. Each agency operates independently and your file from one may contain different information from the others. In this case you may be required to correct inaccurate information on an individual basis.

When you receive copies of your current credit profile(s), make sure that all of the items listed pertain specifically to you. It is not uncommon for a report to contain commingled information on people with the same or similar names, addresses, or social security numbers. In the past, I have seen data appear on my credit report which belonged to my father and although we share the same first and last name, I am a "junior." While it is not uncommon for a credit bureau to make this type of error, it was somewhat unusual because we live in two different states and on opposite ends of the country. Recent litigation has produced industry promises for the elimination of this type of error in the future, but for now, you should continue to examine your credit report carefully for this and other inaccuracies.

In addition to looking for accounts that don't belong to you, check for incorrect or outdated employment data and unfavorable credit information remaining after seven years (bankruptcies remain for ten years). If you should find any misinformation appearing in your report, send the credit agency a letter detailing the inaccuracies along with any evidence to support your claims. After receipt of your request for an investigation, federal law requires the agency to contact the creditor who supplied the questionable information and have them verify its accuracy. If the creditor is unable to do so, the information must be removed from your file. Make sure that the credit bureau sends corrected reports to any and all creditors who obtained a copy of your profile within the preceding six months. You are entitled to this under federal law.

Although the industry claims to complete all investigations in 30 days or less, it may take longer. Be sure to allow adequate time to correct credit inaccuracies prior to applying for your home mortgage loan. It is far better for you to correct any misinformation or add to your report any explanation of minor credit disputes *before* you deal with a lender. By law, you are entitled to add a statement of up to 100 words on your credit report for any disputed claims not corrected at your request. You can be assured that any lender will require you to explain, in writing, any negative information contained in your report prior to considering your request for a loan. By explaining these credit blemishes beforehand, you will demonstrate your willingness to be a responsible, creditworthy individual. This is obviously to your benefit, particularly if you are a borderline credit risk.

The second item that a lender will examine carefully is your employment history and income. The loan officer will look for a stable employment history within the same field or industry for a number of years. If you have changed jobs frequently within the same field during the past several years, most lenders will interpret this as suggesting instability. This factor, then, may reflect negatively on your financial responsibility and character.

Your employment and the income you derive from it will then be verified by contacting your employer. The lender will also request copies of your canceled pay stubs or a recent W-2 Wage and Tax Statement showing withholdings and net pay. If you are self-employed or if your income is derived from sales commissions, the lender will, in most cases, request copies of your tax returns for the previous two years and a copy of a recent profit and loss statement. If you own and operate a small closely held corporation, you will most likely have to provide a copy of your corporate tax return for the past two years as well.

In considering your total gross income, the lender will add your monthly employment income; any secondary income including part-time work or any bonuses or commissions; any alimony or child support; or any other income, such as dividend income, that is consistent and can be substantiated. From these figures, the loan officer will establish a total monthly income.

Now your lender will want you to itemize your fixed monthly overhead expenses. Housing expense will include your present mortgage payments, monthly fire insurance expense (annual payment divided by 12 months), monthly property taxes (add biannual tax payments, then divide by 12), and any mortgage insurance, association dues, or other housing expenses. The person processing your loan will then subtotal these expenditures, add in your approximate monthly utility expenses, and arrive at a total for housing.

Other fixed monthly expenses include alimony or child support payments or any monthly consumer debt payments, such as for an automobile or boat, providing that payments will continue for longer than 10 months. The lender will generally ignore those debts with less than 10 months remaining in payments. If you have any negative cash flow from rental property, this also will be factored in.

Armed with the monthly gross income and expenses totals, your lender will then determine whether or not your monthly "nut" might become too great for you to handle if the additional financing were included. For example, if the lender were to take your total fixed monthly expenses of, say $2,250, and divide it by your current total monthly income of $4,900, the result would indicate that your fixed expenses amount to about 46% of your gross monthly income (2,250 ÷ 4,900 = .46 or 46%). If you were to add the monthly payment on your new financing, let's say $475, to your fixed expenses, your new fixed expenses would be $2,725. Divide this new number by your gross income figure and you come up with 56%.

If your bank has a ceiling limit of 50% expenses/income ratio, it does not necessarily mean that your loan will be rejected, it just means that the lender may not give you as much money as you have requested. The loan officer may need to juggle the loan amount and perhaps lengthen the terms so that your additional payments do not exceed the 50% factor. What the lender would tell you in this scenario is that to meet the institution's criteria, you can only afford another $200 per month in expenses (2,250 + 200 = 2,450 ÷ 4,900 = .50 or 50%). The lender can also insist that in granting the loan you wish, a portion of the proceeds must be withheld to pay off other debt. Such expenses as a car loan or other personal loans may have to be eliminated so you can meet the necessary criteria.

Not all lenders will accept a ceiling of 50% expenses/income ratio; some conservative banks require a much lower ratio. Generally, however, lenders will set an expenses/income ratio of anywhere from 27% to 50%. The ratio used will depend on the type of loan requested and the strength of the borrower's credit. If it is necessary for you to use a higher ratio, you may have to consider dealing with "hard money" lenders; they will usually charge you higher up-front fees and a higher interest rate to obtain your loan. Be sure to ask any lender you are considering to explain the standards used to compute loan eligibility. This will be particularly important if your own computations give you a ratio that is greater than 50%.

The third criterion a lender will use in considering your loan application will be the equity you have in your home. Your lender will be looking for a low loan-to-value ratio. Generally, the lower your LTV percentage, the greater the probability that your application will be considered favorably. As you already know, most lenders will not exceed 75% to 80% LTV. The exception to this is the FHA Title I lending program. If by adding in your proposed financing you compute a factor of considerably less than 75% LTV, there will be greater financial protection for the lender. Remember, however, that most lenders do not wish to find themselves in the position of having to foreclose on your home. For this reason, the LTV factor may be less important than the other two that we have discussed. Most lenders will place a greater emphasis on your credit and employment/income history when considering your application.

UNDERSTANDING AND COMPLETING THE LOAN APPLICATION

To illustrate what a lender will look for when evaluating your application, we will go over and complete the most widely used residential loan application step by step. This type of application is used primarily for new home purchases, refinances, second mortgages, and FHA loans. Some lenders may use their own simplified application for home equity lines of credit and home improvement loans.

Please refer to Figure 3–3 and follow along with the commentary for each portion of the application by matching the assigned number in the figure with its corresponding text explanation.

Loan Application: Items 1–51

1. In most cases, this section will be completed by the lending institution. Unless you are applying for a FHA Title I loan or a VA loan offered for military veterans, your loan will be a conventional loan and this box would be checked.

2. Here again, most lenders will enter the amount for you. For our purposes, you may want to list the amount you are applying for in pencil.

3. Unless you have entered into a "lock-in" on the interest rate, this figure could change before your application is processed and the lender commits to a rate and terms. Since this may change, you will want to pencil in the interest rate you have discussed with your lender.

4. Since your monthly payback schedule may also be altered by the lender, you should enter in the terms that you have

Figure 3–3

Sample Loan Application

RESIDENTIAL LOAN APPLICATION

MORTGAGE APPLIED FOR ►	AMOUNT	INTEREST RATE	NUMBER OF MONTHS	MONTHLY PAYMENT PRINCIPAL & INTEREST	ESCROW/IMPOUNDS (TO BE COLLECTED MONTHLY)
☐ FHA ☐ CO (1) NAL ☐ VA ☐ ______	$ (2)	(3) %	(4)	$ (5)	☐ TAXES ☐ MORTGAGE (6) URANCE ☐ HAZARD INS. ☐ ______

PREPAYMENT OPTION (7)

SUBJECT PROPERTY

PROPERTY STREET ADDRESS	CITY	COUNTY	STATE	ZIP	NO. OF UNITS
(8)					

LEGAL DESCRIPTION (ATTACH DESCRIPTION IF NECESSARY) (9) — YEAR BUILT

PURPOSE OF LOAN: ☐ PURCHASE ☐ CONSTRUCTION · PERMANENT ☐ CONSTRUCTION ☐ REFINANCE ☐ OTHER (EXPLAIN) (10)

Complete this line if Construction-Permanent or Construction Loan ►	LOT VALUE DATA Year Acquired ______	ORIGINAL COST	PRESENT VALUE (A)	COST OF IMPROVEMENTS (B)	TOTAL (A + B)
		$	$	$	$

Complete this line if a Refinance Loan ►	YR. ACQUIRED	ORIGINAL COST	AMT. EXIST. LIENS	PURPOSE OF REFINANCE	DESCRIBE IMPROVEMENTS
(11)		$	$		☐ MADE ☐ TO BE MADE COST: $ ______

SOURCE OF DOWN PAYMENT AND SETTLEMENT CHARGES (12)

TITLE WILL BE HELD IN WHAT NAME(S)	MANNER IN WHICH TITLE WILL BE HELD
(13)	(14)

This application is designed to be completed by the borrower(s) with the lender's assistance. The Co-Borrower Section and all other Co-Borrower questions must be completed and the appropriate box(es) checked if: ☐ Another person will be jointly obligated with the borrower on the loan, or ☐ The Borrower is relying on income from alimony, child support or separate maintenance or on the income or assets of another person as a basis for repayment of the loan, or ☐ The Borrower is married and resides, or the property is located, in a community property state.

BORROWER	CO-BORROWER
NAME (15) — AGE — SCHOOL YEARS ______	NAME (17) — AGE — SCHOOL YEARS ______
PRESENT ADDRESS STREET CITY/STATE/ZIP NUMBER OF YEARS: ______ ☐ OWN ☐ RENT	PRESENT ADDRESS STREET CITY/STATE/ZIP NUMBER OF YEARS: ______ ☐ OWN ☐ RENT
FORMER ADDRESS *(IF LESS THAN 2 YEARS AT PRESENT ADDRESS)* STREET CITY/STATE/ZIP YEARS AT FORMER ADDRESS: ______ ☐ OWN ☐ RENT	FORMER ADDRESS *(IF LESS THAN 2 YEARS AT PRESENT ADDRESS)* STREET CITY/STATE/ZIP YEARS AT FORMER ADDRESS: ______ ☐ OWN ☐ RENT
MARITAL STATUS ☐ MARRIED ☐ SEPARATED ☐ UNMARRIED (INCLUDES SINGLE, DIVORCED, WIDOWED) — DEPENDENTS OTHER THAN LISTED BY CO-BORROWER Number: Ages:	MARITAL STATUS ☐ MARRIED ☐ SEPARATED ☐ UNMARRIED (INCLUDES SINGLE, DIVORCED, WIDOWED) — DEPENDENTS OTHER THAN LISTED BY BORROWER Number: Ages:
NAME AND ADDRESS OF EMPLOYER (16) — NUMBER OF YEARS IN THIS LINE OF WORK OR PROFESSION: ______ YEARS ON THIS JOB: ______ ☐ SELF EMPLOYED *	NAME AND ADDRESS OF EMPLOYER (18) — NUMBER OF YEARS IN THIS LINE OF WORK OR PROFESSION: ______ YEARS ON THIS JOB: ______ ☐ SELF EMPLOYED *
POSITION/TITLE — TYPE OF BUSINESS	POSITION/TITLE — TYPE OF BUSINESS
SOCIAL SECURITY NUMBER — HOME PHONE — BUSINESS PHONE	SOCIAL SECURITY NUMBER — HOME PHONE — BUSINESS PHONE

GROSS MONTHLY INCOME — MONTHLY HOUSING EXPENSE** — DETAILS OF PURCHASE

(19) Item	Borrower	Co-Borrower	Total	(20)	PRESENT	PROPOSED	(21) DO NOT COMPLETE IF REFINANCE	
				Rent	$			
Base Empl. Income	$	$	$	First Mortgage (P&I)		$	a. Purchase Price	$
Overtime				Other Financing (P&I)			b. Total Closing Costs (Est.)	
Bonuses				Hazard Insurance			c. Prepaid Escrows (Est.)	
Commissions				Real Estate Taxes			d. Total (a + b + c)	$
Dividends/Interest				Mortgage Insurance			e. Amount This Mortgage	( )
Net Rental Income				Homeowner Assn. Dues			f. Other Financing	( )
Other † (Before completing, see notice under "DESCRIBE OTHER INCOME" below.)				Other:			g. Other Equity	( )
				Total Monthly Pmt.	$	$	h. Amount of Cash Deposit	( )
				Utilities			i. Closing Costs Paid by Seller	( )
TOTAL	$	$	$	TOTAL	$	$	j. Cash Reqd. for Closing (Est.)	$

DESCRIBE OTHER INCOME

B/C***	DESCRIPTION OF INCOME — Notice: † ALIMONY, CHILD SUPPORT, OR SEPARATE MAINTENANCE INCOME NEED NOT BE REVEALED IF THE BORROWER OR CO-BORROWER DOES NOT CHOOSE TO HAVE IT CONSIDERED AS A BASIS FOR REPAYING THIS LOAN.	MONTHLY AMOUNT
	(22)	$

IF EMPLOYED IN CURRENT POSITION FOR LESS THAN TWO YEARS, COMPLETE THE FOLLOWING

B/C***	PREVIOUS EMPLOYER/SCHOOL	CITY/STATE	TYPE OF BUSINESS	POSITION/TITLE	DATES FROM/TO	MONTHLY INCOME
						$
	(23)					

THESE QUESTIONS APPLY TO BOTH BORROWER AND CO-BORROWER

IF A "YES" ANSWER IS GIVEN TO A QUESTION IN THIS COLUMN, PLEASE EXPLAIN ON AN ATTACHED SHEET.	Borrower Yes or No	Co-Borrower Yes or No
Are there any outstanding judgments against you?		
Have you been declared bankrupt within the past 7 years?		
Have you had property foreclosed upon or given title or deed in lieu thereof in the last 7 years?	(24)	
Are you a party to a law suit?		
Are you obligated to pay alimony, child support, or separate maintenance?		
Is any part of the down payment borrowed?		
Are you a co-maker or endorser on a note?		

	Borrower Yes or No	Co-Borrower Yes or No
Are you a U.S. citizen?		
If "NO," are you a resident alien? (25)		
If "NO," are you a non-resident alien?	(26)	
Explain Other Financing or Other Equity (if any)		

* FHLMC/FNMA require business credit report, signed Federal Income Tax returns for last two years; and, if available, audited Profit and Loss Statement plus balance sheet for same period.
** All Present Monthly Housing Expenses of Borrower and Co-Borrower should be listed on a combined basis. *** Enter "B" for Borrower; "C" for Co-Borrower.

Conforms to requirements of FHLMC 65 and FNMA 1003 Rev. 10/86

Figure 3-3 (continued)

STATEMENT OF ASSETS AND LIABILITIES

THIS STATEMENT AND ANY APPLICABLE SUPPORTING SCHEDULES MAY BE COMPLETED JOINTLY BY BOTH MARRIED AND UNMARRIED CO-BORROWERS IF THEIR ASSETS AND LIABILITIES ARE SUFFICIENTLY JOINED SO THAT THE STATEMENT CAN BE MEANINGFULLY AND FAIRLY PRESENTED ON A COMBINED BASIS. OTHERWISE SEPARATE STATEMENTS AND SCHEDULES ARE REQUIRED (FHLMC 65A/FNMA 1003A). IF THE CO-BORROWER SECTION WAS COMPLETED ABOUT A SPOUSE, THIS STATEMENT AND SUPPORTING SCHEDULES MUST BE COMPLETED ABOUT THAT SPOUSE ALSO.

☐ COMPLETED JOINTLY
☐ NOT COMPLETED JOINTLY

Assets		Liabilities and Pledged Assets

Indicate by (*) those liabilities or pledged assets which will be satisfied upon sale of real estate owned or upon refinancing of the subject property.

DESCRIPTION	CASH OR MARKET VALUE	CREDITORS' NAME, ADDRESS AND ACCOUNT NUMBER		Acct. Name if Not Borrower's	Mo. Pmt. and Mos. Left to Pay		UNPAID BALANCE
					$ PMT	MOS	$
CASH DEPOSIT TOWARD PURCHASE HELD BY (27)	$	INSTALLMENT DEBTS (Include "revolving" charge accounts) (38)	ACCOUNT NO				
CHECKING AND SAVINGS ACCOUNTS (Show names of Institutions and Account Numbers)		Co					
BANK, S&L OR CREDIT UNION (28)		Addr					
		City					
		Co					
Addr		Addr					
City		City					
Acct No		Co					
BANK, S&L OR CREDIT UNION		Addr					
		City					
Addr		Co					
City		Addr					
Acct No		City					
BANK, S&L OR CREDIT UNION		Co					
		Addr					
Addr		City					
City		OTHER DEBTS INCLUDING STOCK PLEDGES (39)					
Acct No							
STOCKS AND BONDS (Number, Description) (29)		REAL ESTATE LOANS (40)					
		Co					
		Addr					
LIFE INSURANCE NET CASH VALUE (30)		City					
Face Amount $		Co					
SUBTOTAL LIQUID ASSETS		Addr					
REAL ESTATE OWNED (Enter Market Value from Schedule of Real Estate Owned) (31)		City					
		AUTOMOBILE LOANS (41)					
VESTED INTEREST IN RETIREMENT FUND (32)		Co					
NET WORTH OF BUSINESS OWNED (Attach Financial Statement) (33)		Addr					
		City					
AUTOMOBILES OWNED (Make and Year) (34)		Co					
		Addr					
		City					
FURNITURE AND PERSONAL PROPERTY (35)		ALIMONY/CHILD SUPPORT/SEPARATE MAINTENANCE OWED TO (42)					
OTHER ASSETS (Itemize) (36)							
		TOTAL MONTHLY PAYMENTS		$ (43)			
TOTAL ASSETS (A) $ (37)		NET WORTH (A minus B) $ (45)		TOTAL LIABILITIES (B) $ (44)			

SCHEDULE OF REAL ESTATE OWNED (If Additional Properties Owned, Attached Separate Schedule)

ADDRESS OF PROPERTY (Indicate S if SOLD, PS if PENDING SALE or R if RENTAL being held for income) (46)	S/PS/R	TYPE OF PROPERTY	PRESENT MARKET VALUE	AMOUNT OF MORTGAGES AND LIENS	GROSS RENTAL INCOME	MORTGAGE PAYMENTS	TAXES, INS. MAINTENANCE AND MISC.	NET RENTAL INCOME
			$	$	$	$	$	$
TOTALS ►			$	$	$	$	$	$

LIST PREVIOUS CREDIT REFERENCES

B/C* (47)	CREDITORS' NAME AND ADDRESS	ACCOUNT NUMBER	PURPOSE	HIGHEST BALANCE	DATE PAID
				$	

LIST ANY ADDITIONAL NAMES UNDER WHICH CREDIT HAS PREVIOUSLY BEEN RECEIVED:

AGREEMENT: The undersigned applies for the loan indicated in this application to be secured by a mortgage, deed of trust or security deed on the property described herein, and represents that the property will not be used for any illegal or restricted purpose, and that all statements made in this application are true and are made for the purpose of obtaining the loan. Verification may be obtained from any source named (48) in this application. The original or a copy of this application will be retained by the lender, even if the loan is not granted.

The undersigned ☐ intend or ☐ do not intend to occupy the property as their primary residence.

I/We fully understand that it is a federal crime punishable by fine or imprisonment, or both, to knowingly make any false statements concerning any of the above facts as applicable under the provisions of Title 18, United States Code, Section 1014.

BORROWER'S SIGNATURE	DATE (49)	CO-BORROWER'S SIGNATURE	DATE

INFORMATION FOR GOVERNMENT MONITORING PURPOSES

The following information is requested by the Federal Government for certain types of loans related to a dwelling, in order to monitor the lender's compliance with equal credit opportunity and fair housing laws. You are not required to furnish this information, but are encouraged to do so. The law provides that a lender may neither discriminate on the basis of this information, nor on whether you choose to furnish it. However, if you choose not to furnish it, under Federal regulations this lender is required to note race and sex on the basis of visual observation or surname. If you do not wish to furnish the above information, please check the box below. (Lender must review the above material to assure that the disclosures satisfy all requirements to which the Lender is subject under applicable state law for the particular type of loan applied for.)

Borrower: ☐ I do not wish to furnish this information.
Co-Borrower: ☐ I do not wish to furnish this information.

Race/National Origin: ☐ American Indian, Alaskan Native ☐ Black (50) ☐ White
☐ Hispanic ☐ Asian, Pacific Islander
☐ Other (specify)
Sex: ☐ Female ☐ Male

Race/National Origin: ☐ American Indian, Alaskan Native ☐ Black ☐ White
☐ Hispanic ☐ Asian, Pacific Islander
☐ Other (specify)
Sex: ☐ Female ☐ Male

TO BE COMPLETED BY INTERVIEWER

This application was taken by:
☐ face to face interview
☐ by mail ☐ by telephone

Interviewer's Signature: _____
Interviewer's Name (Print): _____
Interviewer's Phone Number: _____

ADDRESS OF INTERVIEWER'S EMPLOYER

(51)

*Enter B for Borrower or C for Co-Borrower   REVERSE   Conforms to requirements of FHLMC 65 and FNMA 1003 Rev. 10/86

79

requested in pencil (5 years would be 60 months, 10 years 120 months, etc.).

5. Although you can approximate your amortized payments using the charts provided in Figures 3–1 and 3–2, the bank will calculate the exact monthly payment with their computer. For that reason, you should enter your estimate in pencil.

6. Don't be too concerned with this section. In most cases this will apply only to a purchase of a new home. A lender could require an impound account for such things as taxes or insurance. This would be particularly applicable if a home buyer had less than a 20% down payment applied to a purchase or was otherwise a marginal credit risk.

7. While in most cases a lender will not try to impose an early repayment or prepayment penalty for paying off your loan ahead of schedule, this can be a negotiable point. You must always insist that no penalty be assessed and you should write "No Prepayment Penalty" in the space provided. You want to ensure that the early repayment option is always available to you without negative consequences.

8. Enter the address of the property providing collateral for the loan.

9. This space is for the legal description of the property as listed on the deed to your home. It will read something like: "The Northerly 150 feet measured along the West line of Lot 21 in Block 27 of the Westwood Tract, in the County of Orange, State of California, as per maps recorded in Book 23, Pages 39 to 41, in the office of the county recorder of said county." You probably will not be able to get all this information in the space provided on the form, so simply attach a copy of the description to your application.

10. This is an area of some confusion for people. Many believe that because they are about to undergo "construction" when they remodel their home, they should mark the box labeled "construction." This is incorrect. Construction financing is generally used when a builder or property owner wishes to construct a new dwelling or when substantially remodeling an existing dwelling. In this case, a builder will submit billing directly to the lender for payment of construction expenses

from the borrower's account. By using this method, a lender can assure that the borrowed funds are being used for the specified purpose of construction. Such loans are considered riskier than the more traditional types of financing that we have previously discussed. They can often cost more in fees and carry a higher rate of interest. "Construction–Permanent" is used only when the borrower is refinancing to pay off a short-term construction loan and will generally not apply to home remodeling. Unless your particular situation calls for these types of loans, you needn't concern yourself with them. If your loan is a refinance for the purpose of consolidating your existing financing and providing the money you need for remodeling, mark the appropriate box. If you are applying for a second mortgage, you should also mark the box entitled "Refinance."

11. Complete this section for a refinance and second mortgage: the year you acquired the home, what you paid for it, the total of your existing liens, your purpose for refinancing (remodeling or home improvement). Then describe the improvements in a simplified manner (add a room, remodel kitchen, etc.); indicate that the improvements are to be made and the approximate cost of the improvements (the entire amount of the extra borrowed funds).

12. This item is not applicable to refinance; leave blank or mark "N/A."

13. Indicate whose name(s) is (are) on the title.

14. Indicate in what manner the title is held: Joint Tenants, Tenants-in-Common, etc.

15. Write borrower's name, address if different from property street address; otherwise write "Same as Subject Property"; the rest of this section is self-explanatory.

16. Enter employment information.

17. Provide co-borrower information.

18. Complete co-borrower employment information if relevant.

19. Gross monthly income information is shown here; add category totals to determine a gross monthly income.

20. Enter monthly housing expenses combining both borrower and co-borrower's expenses if you and co-borrower are not living together and both incomes are needed to support the loan. Obtain totals for present expenses and estimate for proposed expenses (in pencil) to determine your own LTV ratio.

21. This section is not applicable to refinance.

22. Describe any other income either you or your co-borrower receive that is not included in your gross monthly income.

23. Requested information is self-explanatory. Here the lender is looking for job stability.

24. You should answer these questions honestly. You can be sure that corresponding information will appear on your credit report. If you entered into bankruptcy but were subsequently discharged, provide the lender with a written statement on all of the circumstances along with a copy of the legal documents discharging you from bankruptcy.

25. This item is self-explanatory.

26. This item only applies to home purchases.

27. This item is not applicable for refinance.

28. List all bank assets, addresses, and account information. Your lender will be sending them all a verification of deposits form to substantiate your claim.

29. List all stocks and bonds you may own and enter current market value.

30. This will apply only to whole life insurance where you have built up annuity position. Term life insurance, which pays only in the event of your death, is not applicable here.

31. Here you will enter the market value of all real estate owned by you and estimated on item 44.

32. List any assets in IRAs (individual retirement accounts) or pension funds.

33. If you own all or part of a business or small corporation, you will want to provide information on its net worth or at least on that portion owned by you. Substantiate your data by providing

the lender with the business's current financial statement, profit and loss statement, and balance sheet. As discussed before, you may be asked to provide two years' tax returns as well.

34. List make, model, and year of all automobiles you now own along with their current estimated market value.

35. Add up the value of your furniture and other personal property.

36. Boats, airplanes, and valuable art objects would all fall under this category. List and estimate market value.

37. Now total all your current assets.

38. Installment debts would include personal loans, credit cards such as MasterCard and Visa, and any store credit cards issued in your name. List only the major ones in the available space. Lenders are not always interested in your gas credit cards unless the amount you owe on them is substantial. If necessary, you may attach an extra sheet of paper if you run out of space.

39. List any other debts you may be responsible for.

40. The lender wants to know the names and addresses of your current mortgage holders. Information on the monthly payment is already accounted for in item 20. Your lender will obtain this information directly from the issuing lender on their Verification of Loan form.

41. This item is self-explanatory.

42. This item is self-explanatory.

43. Add up your total monthly payments not including mortgage payments, which are accounted for under item 20.

44. Total all your unpaid liability balances.

45. To determine your net worth, subtract your total liabilities from your total assets.

46. Provide the information requested on all the real estate that you currently own.

47. Use this section if you have paid off another loan or obligation and can provide a favorable credit reference.

48. This section is very important. Most lenders will charge a higher interest rate for nonowner-occupied property, the theory being that if you are not living in the home, you are not as likely to keep the property in good condition. If you have tenants, they will probably not treat the property with the same respect as you would. This presents a greater risk for the lender, who will want to charge a premium for it. You can't simply tell the lender that you are living in the home either. You can be sure that loan officers will use whatever methods are available to them to verify that what you've written is the truth. Moreover, it is a crime to willfully provide misinformation on the form.

49. Here is where you will provide your signatures.

50. You are not required to complete this section if you do not wish to. Simply mark the box indicated. Be aware that even if you do not choose to provide this information, the lender is required by law to do so based on your appearance. There really is no harm in providing this information willingly as this information is used for the government monitoring purposes referred to on the application.

51. This section will be completed only if your application is taken by a representative of the lender. You do not need to be concerned with it.

OTHER SOURCES OF FINANCING YOUR REMODELING PROJECT

Up to this point we have talked about the most popular methods of financing your project, using your home's equity as collateral for a loan, and the advantages of these methods from a tax standpoint. Now we will concentrate on methods and sources of financing that have no tax advantages. The two exceptions, to be discussed later in the chapter, may be family and "friendly" investors.

Beginning in the taxable year 1991, deductions for personal interest expenses are no longer available, which is certainly a major disadvantage to these types of loans. However, if none of the previously discussed financing methods are an option for you, the money has to come from somewhere.

CONSIDER A PERSONAL LOAN FROM A BANK, CREDIT UNION, OR SAVINGS AND LOAN

Two types of these loans are available, an unsecured personal loan and a collateralized personal loan. As the name implies, an unsecured personal loan is one where the lending institution grants you a loan based solely on your excellent credit, employment/income position, and your personal banking relationship with the lender. Because such loans are not backed by any real or personal property, your approval will be faster than with other types of loans. They can usually be processed in one week or less. You can generally borrow funds from as little as $500 up to a maximum of $25,000, but the repayment terms are very short, usually 3 to 5 years or less. These loans tend to carry a higher interest rate and fees due to the greater risk for the lender. For this reason, I would not recommend this kind of financing unless you are without other viable options. Federally chartered savings and loan associations may be prevented by law from making unsecured loans so you will want to check with them about this.

Collateralized loans, such as passbook loans, are often secured by a certificate of deposit or other savings that you may already have with the lender. You would simply pledge the money you have in savings to guarantee repayment of the obligation. Here again the repayment terms would be fairly short and you would pay from 1% to 3% more in interest than you are currently earning on your savings.

BECOME YOUR OWN BANKER

Since there are no longer any tax benefits on consumer interest deductions, you may want to weigh out the possibility of financing your own loan directly from your savings, and thus avoid having to pay interest to the bank. You could, in effect, pay yourself back with interest on the money you borrow from your own savings. This plan would take discipline but you would definitely save more money in the process.

Why not determine a payback period to yourself of, say, 5 years. Then, using the amortization tables provided in this book, you could compute the monthly payment and write yourself a check every month for that amount. When you pay your other monthly bills, simply deposit that check back into your savings. You would actually increase your savings by paying yourself more than you might otherwise earn on that money. Let me demonstrate how this works.

You need $40,000 for your remodeling project. Actually, you have already saved a little more than that amount but want to hold it in reserve for your children's education. Your oldest child doesn't head off to college for another 5 years, so there is no immediate need for the money. If you paid yourself only 10% interest to borrow that money, it would certainly be a far better deal than the rate your banker would charge you to borrow the same money for which he is currently paying you only 5% (or less) in a savings account. Think about it!

Using the amortization schedule in Figure 3–2, you calculate that the monthly payment on $40,000 amortized for 5 years is approximately $850 ($40 \times 21.25 = \$850$). Every month, as you would on any other bill, you *must* pay that amount and take it as seriously as you would if you knew the lender might foreclose. If you believe that you might be tempted to skip payments to yourself, you probably lack the discipline to handle this responsibility and I do not recommend that you consider this method. If you know you can force yourself to make the payments, this can be an excellent means of "borrowing" the money and increasing your savings at the same time.

USE YOUR CREDIT CARDS S-P-A-R-I-N-G-L-Y

I had some real reservations about including this option for alternative borrowing. While credit cards certainly have their value when it comes to convenience, they are probably the single most financially destructive force in many people's lives. Without proper discipline, credit cards can dig a financial hole from which there is almost no escape.

Allow me to illustrate my point. Let's say that a credit card company has just sent Joe Jones a new "Gold Card" with a $5,000 credit limit. Joe now decides to go out and purchase some building materials for his remodeling project. Before he can believe it, Joe has run up the charges against his card to about $4,950 by the time his very first bill arrives. Since he has nearly reached his credit limit anyway, Joe decides to place his card in a drawer and not use it again until the entire balance is paid off. Oh, if only most people were as disciplined as our friend Joe.

As we have already established, Joe's first bill shows a balance of $4,950. The credit card company has been kind enough to give him some repayment options. Joe may pay anywhere from the minimum of $124 (assuming approximately 2.5% of the balance owing) to the total amount due of $4,950. What does Joe (and many people like him) say? "Let me see here. I can pay either $124 or I can pay anything above that I wish to. Well, I have a lot more things to buy for my project here. Why don't I just pay the minimum until I can get on my feet again. After we're finished here, I can surely pay more." Guess what? Many people, Joe included, never do pay more than the minimum and end up paying far too high a price on the money they borrow.

Joe now mails out his for $124. His new balance is $4,826. Thirty days later, Joe receives his second bill and the balance now owing is $4896.36 ($4,826 principal plus $70.36 interest, at an annual percentage rate of 17.5% or 1.458% monthly. Now Joe's minimum payment is $122, which he pays promptly. His balance now is approximately $4,774.36, but 30 days later with interest added his balance is $4,843.97. As we can plainly see here, Joe is not making very much progress in repaying his loan. What he is doing is paying exorbitantly high interest, which he is unable to deduct from his taxes, on money he might have obtained elsewhere for considerably less.

Make it a rule not to use your credit cards unless you are fully prepared to pay the balance in full when you receive your bill, or at the very least if you only need the money for a very short time and can pay it off in just a few installments. It just doesn't make good financial sense to throw your money away in this manner. By all means, consider some better alternatives first.

ALL IN THE FAMILY: BORROW FROM A FAMILY MEMBER

This may be a tricky area for some of us. You have probably known people who would rather go to the poorhouse than approach a family member about borrowing money; you may even be one of them. Others wouldn't think twice about either borrowing the money from or loaning it to a family member in need. If this is a comfortable alternative to you, I would like to take some time to discuss a sensible method of handling it.

First and foremost, you should treat a borrowing transaction with a family member in a very pragmatic, businesslike fashion. I'm not talking here about wearing a pinstriped suit and carrying a briefcase to meet with your grandmother! No one is a better judge than you about the way you should approach your family to ask for the money. What I'm referring to are the dynamics of structuring the transaction so that it can be beneficial to all parties.

Let's assume that you are talking to your favorite rich uncle, Bob, who is thrilled at the opportunity to assist you financially in your remodeling project. After some preliminary discussion, Uncle Bob expresses some apprehension about having to cash in a six-month certificate of deposit (CD) so that he can give you the money. There will be an interest penalty to him in doing so, and you have no desire to cause him such a financial inconvenience. What if you were to offer him interest of two percentage points above the rate established for the CD? In this way you would be compensating him for his financial inconvenience and still striking a better deal than those available from more traditional lending sources. Don't forget, no fees would be involved in this type of transaction.

Of course, Uncle Bob trusts you implicitly, but you should insist on signing a note. The terms of the note will spell out clearly just how you intend to repay the money and at what interest rate. It is really between the two of you to decide just what is fair. Certainly, for him to earn at least as much as he would have had he invested it in savings is a reasonable starting place. You will also want to make regular monthly payments directly to him until all principal and interest have been repaid.

Now, should you record that note against the title to your property in the form of a second or third trust deed? Of course you should! You will want to deduct that mortgage interest you paid Uncle Bob from your taxes. If you are ever audited by the IRS, it will be clear that you are deducting mortgage interest; whereas without a recording against title, your deduction may be construed as personal interest.

By recording an installment note and trust deed against title (see Figure 3–4 for sample installment note; see also Figure 3–5 for actual recorded instrument), you have made a clean and legitimate transaction that benefits you both. Uncle Bob earns more money than he would have

Figure 3–4

Sample Installment Note Form (Front)

INSTALLMENT NOTE—INTEREST INCLUDED, SECURED BY DEED OF TRUST

$_____   _____, California, _____, 19____

In installments as herein stated, for value received, the undersigned maker(s) promise(s) to pay to _____

_____, or order,

at _____

the sum of _____ DOLLARS.

with interest from _____ on the unpaid principal at the rate of

_____ per cent per annum; principal and interest payable in installments of

_____ Dollars

or more on the _____ day of each _____ month, beginning

on the _____ day of _____

_____

_____

_____

_____ and continuing until said principal and interest have been fully paid.

Each payment shall be credited first to interest then due, and the remainder applied to principal; and interest shall thereupon cease upon the principal so credited. Should default be made in payment of any installment when due, the whole sum of principal and accrued interest shall become immediately due, without notice, at the option of the holder of this note. Interest after maturity will accrue at the rate indicated above. Principal and interest are payable in lawful money of the United States. Each maker will be jointly and severally liable, and consents to the acceptance of security or substituted security for this note, and waives presentment, demand and protest and the right to assert any statute of limitations. A married person who signs this note agrees that recourse may be had against his/her separate property for any obligation contained herein. If any action be instituted on this note, the undersigned promise(s) to pay such sum as the Court may fix as attorney's fees. This Note is secured by a Deed of Trust of even date herewith.

_____   _____

_____   _____

(continued)

Figure 3–4 (continued)

(Back)

PAYMENTS

DATE PAID M D Y			DATE DUE M D Y			AMOUNT PAID	CREDITED ON INT. PRIN.		BALANCE OF PRINCIPAL UNPAID	TO WHOM PAID

Figure 3–5

Sample Deed of Trust Form (Used by permission of Wolcotts, Inc.)

RECORDING REQUESTED BY

WHEN RECORDED MAIL TO

NAME
STREET
ADDRESS
CITY
STATE
ZIP

_____(SPACE ABOVE THIS LINE FOR RECORDER'S USE)_____

DEED OF TRUST AND ASSIGNMENT OF RENTS

THIS DEED OF TRUST, made this _____ day of _____, 19____

BETWEEN _____

_____

_____

_____, herein called Trustor,

whose address is _____
          (Number and Street)   (City)   (State)   (Zip Code)

_____, herein called Trustee, and

_____, herein called Beneficiary.

Trustor irrevocably grants, transfers and assigns to Trustee, in trust, with power of sale, all that real property in the City of _____

_____, County of _____, State of California, described as:

TOGETHER with all the rights, privileges, title and interest which Trustor now has or may hereafter acquire in or to said property, including, without limitation, the rents, issues and profits thereof, and with the appurtenances and all buildings and improvements now or hereafter placed thereon, it being understood and agreed that all classes of property, attached or unattached, used in connection therewith shall be deemed fixtures and subject to the property above described;

SUBJECT, HOWEVER, to the right, power and authority given to and conferred upon Beneficiary hereinbelow to collect and apply such rents, issues and profits;

(For the purposes of this instrument all of the foregoing described real property, property rights and interests shall be referred to as "the property.")

Figure 3–5 (continued)

This Deed of Trust is for the purpose of securing: 1. Payment of the indebtedness in the principal sum of $_____, evidenced by that certain promissory note of even date herewith made by Trustor, or any one of them, payable to Beneficiary or order, and any extension or renewal thereof, which promissory note is substantially in the following form; 2. Performance of each agreement of Trustor contained or incorporated herein by reference; 3. Payment of such sums as may be advanced by Beneficiary or Trustee to protect the security in accordance with the terms of this Deed of Trust, plus interest thereon at the rate set forth in said promissory note; and 4. Payment of such further sums as may be advanced by Beneficiary when evidenced by another promissory note (or promissory notes) reciting it is so secured.

INSTALLMENT NOTE—INTEREST INCLUDED, SECURED BY DEED OF TRUST

$_____   _____, California, _____, 19____

In installments as herein stated, for value received, the undersigned maker(s) promise(s) to pay to _____

_____, or order,

at _____

the sum of _____ DOLLARS,

with interest from _____ on the unpaid principal at the rate of

_____ per cent per annum; principal and interest payable in installments of

_____ Dollars

or more on the _____ day of each _____ month, beginning

on the _____ day of _____

_____

_____

_____

_____ and continuing until said principal and interest have been fully paid.

Each payment shall be credited first to interest then due, and the remainder applied to principal; and interest shall thereupon cease upon the principal so credited. Should default be made in payment of any installment when due, the whole sum of principal and accrued interest shall become immediately due, without notice, at the option of the holder of this note. Interest after maturity will accrue at the rate indicated above. Principal and interest are payable in lawful money of the United States. Each maker will be jointly and severally liable, and consents to the acceptance of security or substituted security for this note, and waives presentment, demand and protest and the right to assert any statute of limitations. A married person who signs this note agrees that recourse may be had against his/her separate property for any obligation contained herein. If any action be instituted on this note, the undersigned promise(s) to pay such sum as the Court may fix as attorney's fees. This Note is secured by a Deed of Trust of even date herewith.

_____   _____

_____   _____

To protect the security of this Deed of Trust, Trustor agrees:

(1) To keep the property in good condition and repair; not to remove, substantially alter or demolish any building thereon; to complete or restore promptly and in good and workmanlike manner any building which may be constructed, damaged or destroyed thereon and to pay when due all claims for labor performed and materials furnished therefor; to comply with all laws affecting the property or requiring any alterations or improvements to be made thereon; not to commit or permit waste thereof; not to commit, suffer or permit any act upon the property in violation of law; to cultivate, irrigate, fertilize, fumigate, prune and do all other acts which from the character or use of the property may be reasonably necessary, the specific enumerations herein not excluding the general.

(2) To provide, maintain and deliver to Beneficiary fire, and if required by Beneficiary, other insurance satisfactory to and with loss payable to Beneficiary. The amount collected under any fire or other insurance policy may be applied by Beneficiary upon any indebtedness secured hereby and in such order as Beneficiary may determine, or at option of Beneficiary the entire amount so collected or any part thereof may be released to Trustor. Such application or release shall not cure or waive any default or notice of default hereunder or invalidate any act done pursuant to such notice.

(3) To appear in and defend any action or proceeding purporting to affect the security hereof or the rights or powers of Beneficiary or Trustee; and to the extent permitted by law, to pay all costs and expenses, including the cost of evidence of title and attorney's fees, in any such action or proceeding in which Beneficiary or Trustee may appear, and in any suit brought by Beneficiary to foreclose this Deed of Trust or enforce the rights of Beneficiary or Trustee hereunder.

(4) To pay: at least ten days before delinquency all taxes and assessments affecting the property, including assessments on appurtenant water stock; when due, all encumbrances, charges and liens, with interest, on the property or any part thereof, which appear to be prior or superior hereto; and all costs, fees and expenses of this Trust to the extent permitted by law.

(5) Should Trustor fail to make any payment or to do any act as herein provided, then Beneficiary or Trustee, but without obligation to do so, and without notice to or demand upon Trustor, and without releasing Trustor from any obligation hereof, may: make or do the same in such manner and to such extent as either may deem necessary to protect the security hereof, Beneficiary or Trustee being authorized to enter upon the property for such purposes; appear in and defend any action or proceeding purporting to affect the security hereof or the rights or powers of Beneficiary or Trustee; pay, purchase, contest or compromise any encumbrance, charge or lien which in the judgment of either appears to be prior or superior hereto; and, in exercising any such powers, pay necessary expenses, employ counsel and pay his reasonable fees.

(6) To pay immediately and without demand all sums expended by Beneficiary or Trustee pursuant to the terms of this Deed of Trust, with interest from date of expenditure at the rate set forth in the aforesaid promissory note.

(7) That any award of damages in connection with any condemnation for public use of or injury to said property or any part thereof is hereby assigned and shall be paid to Beneficiary who may apply or release such moneys received by him in the same manner and with the same effect as above provided for disposition of proceeds of fire or other insurance.

(8) That by accepting payment of any sum secured hereby after its due date, Beneficiary does not waive his right either to require prompt payment when due of all other sums so secured or to declare default for failure so to pay.

Figure 3–5 (continued)

(9) That at any time, or from time to time, without liability therefor and without notice, upon written request of Beneficiary and presentation of this Deed of Trust and said promissory note for endorsement, and without affecting the personal liability of any person for payment of the indebtedness secured hereby, Trustee may: reconvey any part of the property; consent to the making of any map or plat thereof; join in granting any easement thereon; or join in any extension agreement or any agreement subordinating the lien or charge hereof.

(10) That upon written request of Beneficiary stating that all sums secured hereby have been paid, and upon surrender of this Deed of Trust and said promissory note to Trustee for cancellation and retention and upon repayment of its fees, Trustee shall reconvey, without warranty, the property then held hereunder. The recitals in such reconveyance of any matters or facts shall be conclusive proof of the truthfulness thereof. The grantee in such reconveyance may be described as ''the person or persons legally entitled thereto.''

(11) That as additional security, Trustor hereby gives to and confers upon Beneficiary the right, power and authority, during the continuance of these Trusts, to collect the rents, issues and profits of the property, reserving unto Trustor the right, prior to any default by Trustor in payment of any indebtedness secured hereby or in performance of any agreement hereunder, to collect and retain such rents, issues and profits as they become due and payable. Upon any such default, Beneficiary may at any time without notice, either in person, by agent, or by a receiver to be appointed by a court, and without regard to the adequacy of any security for the indebtedness hereby secured, enter upon and take possession of the property or any part thereof, in his own name sue for or otherwise collect such rents, issues and profits, including those past due and unpaid, and apply the same, less costs and expenses of operation and collection, including reasonable attorney's fees, upon any indebtedness secured hereby, and in such order as Beneficiary may determine. The entering upon and taking possession of the property, the collection of such rents, issues and profits and the application thereof as aforesaid, shall not cure or waive any default or notice of default hereunder or invalidate any act done pursuant to such notice.

(12) That upon default by Trustor in payment of any indebtedness secured hereby or in performance of any agreement hereunder, Beneficiary may declare all sums secured hereby immediately due and payable by delivery to Trustee of written declaration of default and demand for sale and of written notice of default and of election to cause to be sold the property, which notice Trustee shall cause to be filed for record. Beneficiary also shall deposit with Trustee this Deed of Trust, said promissory note and all documents evidencing expenditures secured hereby.

After the lapse of such time as may then be required by law following the recordation of said notice of default, and notice of sale having been given as then required by law, Trustee, without demand on Trustor, shall sell said property at the time and place fixed by it in said notice of sale, either as a whole or in separate parcels, and in such order as it may determine, at public auction to the highest bidder for cash in lawful money of the United States, payable at time of sale. Trustee may postpone sale of all or any portion of said property by public announcement at such time and place of sale, and from time to time thereafter may postpone such sale by public announcement at the time fixed by the preceding postponement. Trustee shall deliver to such purchaser its deed conveying the property so sold, but without any covenant or warranty, express or implied. The recitals in such deed of any matters or facts shall be conclusive proof of the truthfulness thereof. Any person, including Trustor, Trustee, or Beneficiary as hereinafter defined, may purchase at such sale.

After deducting all costs, fees and expenses of Trustee and of this Trust to the extent permitted by law, including the cost of evidence of title in connection with such sale, Trustee shall apply the proceeds of sale to payment of: all sums expended under the terms hereof, not then repaid, with accrued interest at the rate set forth in the aforesaid promissory note; all other sums then secured hereby; and the remainder, if any, to the person or persons legally entitled thereto.

Immediately after such sale, Trustor shall surrender possession of the property to the purchaser, in the event possession has not previously been surrendered by Trustor, and upon failure to vacate the property, Trustor shall pay to the purchaser the reasonable rental value of the property, and/or at purchaser's option, may be dispossessed in accordance with the law applicable to tenant's holding over.

(13) That Trustor, or if the property shall have been transferred, the then record owner, together with Beneficiary, may from time to time, by instrument in writing, substitute a successor or successors to any Trustee named herein or acting hereunder, which instrument, executed and acknowledged by each and recorded in the office of the recorder of the county or counties where the property is situated, shall be conclusive proof of proper substitution of such successor Trustee or Trustees, who shall, without conveyance from the Trustee predecessor, succeed to all its title, estate, rights, powers and duties. Said instrument must contain the name of the original Trustor, Trustee and Beneficiary hereunder, the book and page where this Deed is recorded, the name and address of the new Trustee, and such other matters as may be required by law. If notice of default shall have been recorded, this power of substitution cannot be exercised until after the costs, fees and expenses of the then acting Trustee shall have been paid to such Trustee, who shall endorse receipt thereof upon such instrument of substitution. The procedure herein provided for substitution of Trustees shall be exclusive of all other provisions for substitution, statutory or otherwise, to the extent permitted by law.

(14) That this Deed of Trust applies to, inures to the benefit of, and binds all parties hereto, their heirs, legatees, devisees, administrators, executors, successors and assigns. The term Beneficiary shall mean the owner and holder, including pledgees, of the promissory note secured hereby, whether or not named as Beneficiary herein. In this Deed of Trust, whenever the context so requires, the masculine gender includes the feminine and/or neuter, and the singular number includes the plural, and all obligations of each Trustor hereunder are joint and several.

(15) That Trustee accepts this Trust when this Deed of Trust, duly executed and acknowledged, is made a public record as provided by law. Trustee is not obligated to notify any party hereto of pending sale under any other Deed of Trust or of any action or proceeding in which Trustor, Beneficiary or Trustee shall be a party unless brought by Trustee.

(16) Without affecting the liability of Trustee or of any other party now or hereafter bound by the terms hereof for any obligation secured hereby, Beneficiary may, from time to time and with or without notice as he shall determine, release any person now or hereafter liable for the performance of such obligation, extend the time for payment or performance, accept additional security, and alter, substitute or release any security.

(17) Trustee or Beneficiary may enter upon and inspect the premises at any reasonable time.

(18) No remedy hereby given to Beneficiary or Trustee is exclusive of any other remedy hereunder or under any present or future law. No delay on the part of Trustee or Beneficiary in enforcing their respective rights or remedies hereunder shall constitute a waiver thereof.

(19) Trustor waives the right to assert at any time any statute of limitations as a bar to any action brought to enforce any obligation hereby secured.

(20) Should Trustor, without Beneficiary's written consent, voluntarily sell, transfer or convey his interest in the property or any part thereof, or if by operation of law, it be sold, transferred or conveyed, then Beneficiary may, at its option, declare all sums secured hereby immediately due and payable. Consent to one such transaction shall not be deemed to be a waiver of the right to require such consent to future or successive transactions.

(21) The invalidity or unenforceability of any provision herein shall not affect the validity and enforceability of any other provision.

Each undersigned Trustor requests that a copy of any Notice of Default and of any Notice of Sale hereunder shall be mailed to him at the address hereinabove set forth.

_____   _____

_____   _____

STATE OF CALIFORNIA   } ss.

COUNTY OF _____

On this _____ day of _____, in the year 19____,
before me, the undersigned, a Notary Public in and for said State, personally appeared _____

personally known to me (or proved to me on the basis of satisfactory evidence) to be the person__ whose name__ _____ subscribed to the within instrument, and acknowledged to me that __he__ executed it.

WITNESS my hand and official seal.

_____

Notary Public in and for said State.

Figure 3–5 (continued)

——————————————————— **DO NOT RECORD** ———————————————————

REQUEST FOR FULL RECONVEYANCE

To be used only when note has been paid.

To _____, Trustee   Dated_____

The undersigned is the legal owner and holder of all indebtedness secured by the within Deed of Trust. All sums secured by said Deed of Trust have been fully paid and satisfied, and you are hereby requested and directed, on payment to you of any sums owing to you under the terms of said Deed of Trust, to cancel all evidences of indebtedness secured by said Deed of Trust delivered to you herewith, together with said Deed of Trust, and to reconvey, without warranty, to the parties designated by the terms of said Deed of Trust, the estate now held by you thereunder.

MAIL RECONVEYANCE TO:

_____   _____

_____   _____

Do not lose or destroy this Deed of Trust OR THE NOTE which it secures.
Both must be delivered to the Trustee for cancellation before reconveyance will be made.

Before you use this form, read it, fill in all blanks, and make whatever changes are appropriate and necessary to your particular transaction. Consult a lawyer if you doubt the form's fitness for your purpose and use. Wolcotts makes no representation or warranty, express or implied, with respect to the merchantability or fitness of this form for an intended use or purpose.

Wolcotts forms can be found in most good office supply or stationery stores.

with a CD, and you have obtained a very favorable borrowing arrangement with fully deductible interest. I assume, of course, that you meet the tax deductibility criteria discussed earlier in this chapter.

By insisting that you and Uncle Bob approach this transaction in a businesslike fashion, you stand a greater chance of not having the loan interfere with your relationship. Everyone certainly has the best of intentions and expectations when they enter into a borrowing and lending arrangement with a family member. These very same intentions and expectations can turn to disaster if the payments stop and the agreement falls apart. Protecting the interests of the lender, even if the person insists that it isn't necessary because of your relationship, has a way of keeping everybody talking if things go sour. Most people would be less inclined to default on their obligation if the relative's ultimate recourse was to foreclose on their property. It is important to treat this type of loan with the same responsibility that you would have toward money borrowed from a bank.

FIND A "FRIENDLY" INVESTOR

To establish just who a "friendly" investor really is, let us first establish who a friendly investor is not. A friendly investor is not someone who has a secret desire to own your home through foreclosure. You certainly don't want to be so eager to get the remodeling project underway that you find yourself dealing with a "hard" money lender whose rates and terms make it too difficult for you to keep up with the payments. Just be cautious in your dealings and maintain your objectivity.

Find a friend or ask around for someone looking to make a fair return on their investment. Approach these people in much the same way as you would a family member. Find some common ground with respect to rates and terms and negotiate a workable arrangement. Here again, you should record the note and trust deed against title as a guarantee to the investor, and so that you may cleanly deduct the mortgage interest you pay from your taxes.

The most common procedure for recording this note and deed of trust against the title to your home requires that you complete a form similar to the one illustrated in Figure 3–5, have your signature notarized, and then visit your county's hall of records where you will pay a small recording fee to have the document legally recorded. You may want to check with your county offices to verify the procedure required in your area. These forms should be available at a legal stationery store or from a title insurance company with offices located in your area.

STAY AWAY FROM CONTRACTOR FINANCING

Obtaining financing from your contractor is a mistake in my view. Without any intention of overgeneralizing here, I believe that this type of borrowing does not serve your best interests.

Some larger contractors can often arrange financing either through their own organizational structure ("in house") or by outside banking resources. These loans have a tendency to be more expensive in terms of rates and fees. Contractors will also generally pocket some of these fees, which they are legally entitled to do, for their time in making arrangements for this loan. Furthermore, since they have no personal fiduciary responsibility to you for arranging the lowest rates, you are pretty much placed in a "take it or leave it" position. There are better alternatives available to you, and I have mentioned most of them.

REVIEW

- Refinance your first mortgage to include remodeling funds if you calculate that lower interest outweighs loan costs (fees).

- Obtain a second mortgage for short-term borrowing and save interest expenses.

- Use a home equity line of credit so you don't borrow the funds until they are actually needed.

- Consider a home improvement loan for small remodeling projects (under $25,000).

- Use an FHA Title I home improvement loan if you have little or no equity and have exhausted other options.

- Familiarize yourself with the favorable tax treatment for home mortgage interest deductions.

- Understand what mortgage lenders will be looking for and how to complete the application forms.

- Consider obtaining a personal loan to fund your project.

- Loan the money to yourself if possible for a forced savings program.

- Use your credit cards with restraint.

- Talk to a family member about a loan and treat it as if it were any other business borrowing transaction.

- Look for a friendly investor willing to deal with you.

- If possible, avoid contractor financing.

Hire a "Builder," Not a "Contractor"

The word *contractor* can be defined as "one of the parties to a contract." To my way of thinking, this definition implies that a contractor is perhaps more skilled in the art of drafting contracts than in doing the work you want done. A *builder,* on the other hand, is commonly defined as "a person in the business of constructing buildings." Which would you prefer to hire?

Contracts are, of course, an important part of any remodeling project, but some "contractors" seem to be more interested in their contractual agreement (i.e., how much and when they are going to get paid) than in seeing to it that you get the best job for the money you are willing to pay. It is this type of "contractor" you will want to avoid. Hire a professional builder and you will recognize the distinction. This is my first rule for successful remodeling: Always hire "professionals."

HINTS FOR HIRING PROFESSIONALS

In any field, professionals are usually harder to find than those who are, shall we say, "less than" professional. Since the skills of the true professionals in any field tend to be highly respected, they are usually in great demand and many people are willing to wait for them. Generally speaking, those who are less professional seem to be more available and will often come searching for you.

The really good builders and tradesmen generally don't have to do much advertising because their work speaks for itself. These professionals work almost exclusively through referrals, that is from people who were satisfied with their work and tell their friends or neighbors about it. These people take pride in their work and genuinely want you to be satisfied with the job they've done.

Builders who are less professional may not be as concerned with the quality of the work they perform for you because they don't count on your satisfaction for their next job. They have already moved on and are knocking on new doors to hustle their next job. It is because they may knock on your door next that I have written my second rule for successful remodeling: Never hire anyone who comes to you looking for work.

Unfortunately, I learned this rule the hard way. One day, when the house I was remodeling was all torn up and it was obvious to all who drove by that construction was underway, a young man knocked on the door. He introduced himself as a drywalling contractor and asked if he might bid on the job. I figured that I would have nothing to lose by at least showing him the job and permitting him to quote a price.

The price he offered indicated that using him would save a considerable amount of money. He had references, but unfortunately these other jobs were in progress and there was no way to see the final product. Since drywall is not the most complex of construction phases and there is little chance of really messing it up because any flaws are usually easy to see, I decided to hire him.

As it turned out, I ended up having to spend a great deal more of my time directing the job than I should have, even having to help move large pieces of drywall myself because the subcontractor failed to send enough people for the job. He then failed to pay some of his workers, forcing me to intercede and delaying the work considerably. His own attendance at the job site was spotty at best. The money saved by hiring this unreliable person was not worth the added time and aggravation.

The lessons to be learned from this bad experience are clear. First, as I've already mentioned, never hire anyone off the street who comes to you looking for work. Second, *though you don't always get what you pay for if you pay more, you almost always get what you pay for if you pay less than the amount that the job should cost.* And finally, always hire the person who has experience and the references to back it up.

THINGS TO LOOK OUT FOR WHEN CHECKING REFERENCES

To really understand what to look for or to look out for when checking references, it is important to put yourself on the other end of the line. Imagine for a moment that someone you do not know is calling you to ask about a builder who has worked on your project. This person will certainly ask you some of the following questions, or perhaps all of them:

1. Has [subcontractor's name] done some work for you?

2. What did this subcontractor do for you?

3. Were you satisfied with the workers' job performance?

4. Would you hire this subcontractor again?

5. Did the subcontractor's crew show up for work on time?

6. Was the job finished on schedule?

7. Did the workers keep the job site fairly clean?

8. Did the subcontractor work well with you; was he easy to get along with?

9. Would you recommend this subcontractor to me or others?

10. Is there anything else that you think we should know about the subcontractor?

These are the same questions that you should ask when you check references. I'm sure that you can probably think of some others as well, but let's start with these.

If you have been thoroughly satisfied with the job that the subcontractor did for you, giving a good reference is easy. You will sound enthusiastic, and you will suffer from no loss of words when describing how happy you were with the work. But what if you were less than totally satisfied? How then would you respond to these same questions?

There are different philosophies on how best to answer such inquiries honestly if you were not happy; I will discuss one good approach here. You will, of course, want to choose the approach that works best for you.

The subcontractor obviously chose to use me as a reference because he thought I was satisfied with his work and was sure that I would provide a good reference for him. In this particular case, let's assume that the subcontractor has a family to support and this is how he has chosen to earn his living. And finally, I want to be very careful not to hurt this person because my project may not have been indicative of his general performance; the work, for example, could have presented certain problems that were not inherent in his other jobs.

So now what do I do? A potential customer of the subcontractor is asking me questions about his work when I am not a completely satisfied customer. I don't want to lie and tell him what a great subcontractor I thought he was, but should I be completely honest and tell him what I really thought about this guy's work? My answer to that is yes and not completely. If I believed that the subcontractor was a crook and had done an absolutely terrible job, my answer would simply be yes. Nothing can be gained from allowing someone to continue ripping people off with shoddy workmanship. However, if this subcontractor believed that I thought he had done a bad job, then why in the world would he have a prospective customer call me when I could conceivably blow the deal for him? He, at least, thought he had done a good job.

In this case, I would try to limit my answers to the specific questions that were asked. In other words, if someone asked me if I was satisfied with the job performance, I might respond by emphasizing the areas in which I thought he performed well. "He always showed up on a workday and was pleasant to work with." "He did a good job of sticking to a schedule and finished only a little beyond his original completion date." "He helped me by providing a useful list of subcontractors." "He did his best and always tried to do the job right."

This doesn't mean I would try to sugarcoat the truth. If the person asked more specifically about certain aspects of the job, I would answer them truthfully. For example, if someone were to ask me to describe the subcontractor's weak points, I might say: "Well, my finish carpenter did have trouble with the door frames because they were not quite level (the framing contractor's responsibility), but you just have to make sure that he takes his time and does it right." As to the question about whether or not we would hire the subcontractor again, I might respond in this way: ". . . Our job was very difficult to do and I'm not sure that anyone could have done a better job . . . we might hire him again." This was a truthful and fair response and would probably not result in his losing the job.

Since this is how a fairly typical person would respond to a reference call, you now know what to listen for when you are on the asking end. Are the references you are calling upbeat and enthusiastic about the subcontractor's work? Are they at no loss for words when expressing their happiness with the person? Can they admit without hesitation that they would hire the subcontractor again? If not—if their answers seem evasive or uncertain—then you had better ask more specific questions and weigh your decision very carefully before hiring this particular subcontractor.

I recommend that you obtain at least three to four recent references and by all means ask to see the work that the subcontractor has completed. If you are not getting the kind of answers you want but still consider hiring the person, ask for several more references. If the subcontractor has left a trail of mostly happy customers, he will have no problem providing them to you. If he has difficulty fulfilling your request, you may be talking to his friends and relatives and are less likely to get an unbiased perspective.

One other suggestion for checking out a prospective subcontractor is to contact the licensing agency that governs your state's contractors. If your prospect carries a legitimate contractor's license, this agency can provide you with valuable information. They can tell you the "class" (i.e., general contractor, plumber, etc.) of the license held, how long the person has been in business, the address of the licensee, the charter expiration date, whether the person is considered to be "a contractor in good standing," and/or whether he has had any complaints or disputes filed against him.

Just remember to do your homework in advance and make intelligent inquiries about the persons whom you consider hiring. Though it may be impossible to avoid problems completely, you should do as much as possible in advance to limit them.

OBTAIN AT LEAST THREE BIDS

As I mentioned before, it is essential that you obtain at least three bids from three different "subs" (subcontractors) for each phase of the building project. By doing this, you will have a pretty good idea of what it should cost to do the work.

To ensure that all prices received are competitive with one another, be sure to spell out exactly what each bidder will be expected to do. All three bids *should* be fairly close to each other. If any appear to be either very high or very low, then they should probably not be considered.

It is often said that "experts" suggest you should always take the middle bid. I don't necessarily agree with this advice for two reasons. The first is that you should not, on the basis of cost alone, dismiss your "gut" feeling about hiring someone. I have sometimes hired the highest bidder because I had good feelings about the person and his air of professionalism; I was sure the extra cost would represent money well spent, and it almost always turned out to be a good decision. This is not to say that in all cases the more you pay, the more satisfied you will be. Just remember that you must also allow your instinct to play an important role in your decision-making process.

The second reason for not always taking the middle bid is that the low bidder may not have the same overhead expenses as the middle one. Both subs may be equally competent, but one may have to apply more of his costs to his expenses. These costs are a price of doing business, and this bidder must recoup them to survive financially. The lower bidder may have fewer overhead expenses and can therefore offer you a better price. You should consider other factors when choosing the bid that is best for you.

NEGOTIATING FOR COSTS: YOUR MONEY AS THE COMMODITY

One thing that always amazes me when I hear about people negotiating for costs is their apparent lack of common sense. To illustrate my point, let me stage a mock discussion between a hypothetical owner-builder (OB) and a subcontractor he wants to hire. The comments within parentheses represent the thoughts of each individual.

SUB: For all the work you need done here, my price is $8,500. (And that's a good price considering all I have to do! Should I have charged more?)

OB: (I'll bet I can get this guy to take $8,000 easily and he'll be darn glad to get it! After all, these guys expect a little negotiating. He'll go along, I'm sure he needs the work!) Oh gee, I really only have $8,000 in the budget for this particular project. Do you think you could live with that!

SUB: (Hey, what's this guy trying to pull on me? I gave him a fair price and now he's trying to beat me out of $500? How am I going to meet my expenses and still have a little profit left over for myself? After all, I've got to feed my family too!) I . . . I really don't know. There is a lot of work here and that really is a fair price for all that I will have to do.

OB: (I got him on the ropes now! He'll go for it if he knows what's good for him.) Well, I'm sorry. That's all I can really afford to spend. Take $8,000 and the job is yours. Otherwise, I'll just have to find someone else who can do it for that price.

SUB: (I really do need the work. Maybe I can cut a few corners here and there to make up the difference. I'm not really very happy with this guy but if he wants an $8,000 job, he's going to get one.) Okay, I'll do it for $8,000.

OB: Great, let's get started! (What a great negotiator I am. I just saved myself 500 bucks!)

Remember that the sub will do a better job if he is satisfied that he will earn enough to make a fair profit. If he has a bad attitude going into the work, it will likely reflect in his approach to the job.

It is important to look at your money as the commodity in any negotiation for costs. Many people forget this when they shop. They tend to think that their need to have the item they wish to purchase is greater than the seller's need to have their money. Although this is simply not true, most people are conditioned to believe that it is. What you need to do is convince the person you are negotiating with that he needs your money more than you need his services.

Here is an alternative method of handling that same hypothetical negotiation using your new strategy:

OB: Thank you for taking the time to look at my job. I'm sure you are very busy with other projects. (I've made him feel important and let him know that I appreciate his time. After all, if he doesn't get the job, he has no way to get paid for the time he has spent bidding on my project. No one likes to work for free.) Before you bid on our project, I would like to explain a few things. First of all, I understand that the bid you will be giving me will represent the very best price you can offer for the work that needs to be done. I also want you to know, right off the bat, that I have never attempted to try and negotiate a better price once a person has given me his quote. After all, I expect you to make what you need to have to make the job worth your time. In fairness to you, however, I must also tell you that I will be getting a total of three bids for this particular phase of the job. Unfortunately, we are really working under a very tight budget on this project, and although cost is not our only concern, I sincerely hope we can reach an agreement that will give you what you will need and still provide us with your very best work.

Now, what have we said here? Have we insulted this person or made him feel that we are trying to cheat him out of his money? No. We have treated him with respect and have truthfully laid all our cards on the table. With any luck, we have instilled a sense of mutual trust, which is the key to starting any good working relationship. It's now up to him to decide what he wishes to do with the information we have given him. He may decide not to make a bid if he likes to take only those jobs where he can charge whatever he chooses without challenge. At least you have avoided wasting each other's valuable time. Or, he may decide to bid and, in the process, be much more careful that he has made accurate calculations and has clearly spelled out the scope of the work that he will perform. What more can you ask for? In a sincere way, you have told him what he can expect from you and have asked the same of him in return. You have safeguarded your money—your commodity if you will—you have demonstrated your leadership skills, and in the process, you have not sacrificed the quality of the work to be performed. Well done!

ESTABLISHING THE GROUND RULES

Once you have selected the best bid for your job, contacted this sub's references, and are satisfied with your choice, it is time to establish the ground rules.

These ground rules may not necessarily take the form of a formal written contract between you and the sub, though I do generally recommend it. The contract should spell out simply but clearly all the responsibilities of each party to the agreement. It is important for the parties to have a mutual understanding *before* any work is performed or any expenses are incurred. If all goes well and everyone is satisfied, you will never have to refer to this document again. It is only when a dispute arises that you each may need a reminder of your initial agreement.

The contract need not be written in overly technical "legalese" in which every possible contingency is covered. Remember, you are hiring a "builder" (or plumber, or electrician, or whatever description fits) not a "contractor." You shouldn't have to be a lawyer, nor should you have to hire one to prepare your agreement. The agreement will be invoked only if communications completely break down between you and your sub.

In some cases a subcontractor will prepare, often as part of his bid, a simple contract that will require nothing more than your review and a signed approval (see sample contract, Figure 4–1). Other subs will insist on a more formal contract (see sample standard contracts, Figures 4–2 and 4–3).

As you can see from these samples, the contracts are generally designed to protect both sides to the agreement. Be aware, however, that since they have been prepared and provided by the builder, they may favor his interests. It is perfectly acceptable for you to attach an addendum to the contract stipulating whatever you would like to cover in the agreement. Some sample items you may find it advantageous to include are illustrated in Figure 4–4. This is by no means a complete list. You can add anything you wish to the addendum provided both parties agree and both sign the document.

The addendum should include a stipulation that the tradesman will provide a certificate of insurance as proof of his coverage for workers' compensation and liability. You should stipulate that this certificate must

Figure 4–1

Sample Contract

XYZ CONSTRUCTION CORP.
STATE LICENSE NO. 123456
ADDRESS
PHONE

PROPOSAL AND CONTRACT:

Date:

Proposal Submitted To: (Name, Address, Phone)

Work to be performed at: (Job Address)

We hereby propose to furnish the materials and perform the labor necessary for the completion of: Work description

_____

_____

_____

_____

All of the above described work to be performed in a substantial and workmanlike manner in accordance with standard practices of the industry for the sum of:
$_____ payable 1/3 upon delivery of materials; 1/3 upon completion
of _____; and 1/3 upon satisfactory completion.

Any alterations or deviations from the above specifications involving extra costs, will be executed only upon written orders, and will become an extra charge over and above the estimate. All agreements contingent upon strikes, accidents or delays beyond our control. Owner to carry fire, tornado and other necessary insurance upon above work. Worker's Compensation and Public Liability Insurance on the above work to be taken out by: _____

This proposal may be withdrawn by us if not accepted within: _____ days.

ACCEPTANCE
The above prices, specifications and conditions are satisfactory and are hereby accepted. You are authorized to do the work as specified. Payment will be made as outlined above.

Date: _____   **Signature:** _____

Figure 4–2

Sample Proposal and Contract Form (Used by permission of Wolcotts, Inc.)

PROPOSAL AND CONTRACT FOR HOME IMPROVEMENT*

Date: _____, 19____ **TO** _____

_____, (hereinafter "Owner"), Telephone no. ( )_____ :

_____(hereinafter "Contractor")

propose(s) to furnish all materials and perform all labor necessary to complete the following: [Insert a description of the work to be done and a description of the materials to be used and the equipment to be used or installed, and state the address of the job site.]

All of the above work is to be completed in a substantial and workmanlike manner according to standard practices for the sum of _____

_____ Dollars ($).

Progress payments to be made as follows and in accordance with the terms and conditions of paragraph 1 on the reverse side:

Amount of Work or Services to be Performed or Description of any Materials or Equipment to be Supplied	Amount of Payment (Must be shown as a sum in dollars and cents)

The remaining balance of the contract is to be paid within _____ days after completion.

This proposal is valid until _____, and if accepted on or before that date, work will commence approximately on _____ and will be substantially completed approximately on _____, subject to delays caused by acts of God, stormy weather, uncontrollable labor trouble, or unforeseen contingencies.

The following constitutes substantial commencement of work pursuant to this proposal and contract: [Specify]

> **FAILURE BY CONTRACTOR WITHOUT LAWFUL EXCUSE TO SUBSTANTIALLY COMMENCE WORK WITHIN TWENTY (20) DAYS FROM THE APPROXIMATE DATE SPECIFIED IN THIS PROPOSAL AND CONTRACT WHEN WORK WILL BEGIN IS A VIOLATION OF THE CONTRACTORS LICENSE LAW.**

Any alteration or deviation from the above specifications, including but not limited to any such alteration or deviation involving additional material and/or labor costs, will be executed only upon a written order for same, signed by Owner and Contractor, and if there is any charge for such alteration or deviation, the additional charge will be added to the contract price of this contract.

If any payment is not made when due, Contractor may suspend work on the job until such time as all payments due have been made. A failure to make payment for a period in excess of _____ days from the due date of the payment shall be deemed a material breach of this contract.

Respectfully submitted,

> **NOTICE TO OWNER OR TENANT:** You have the right to require Contractor to have a performance and payment bond.

Name and Registration No. of any Salesperson who solicited or negotiated this contract:

Name: _____ No. _____

By _____
Name of Contractor

_____
Signature

_____
Street Address

City   State   Zip   ( )   Telephone No

Contractor's State License No

ACCEPTANCE

You are hereby authorized to furnish all materials and labor required to complete the work mentioned in this Proposal, for which I/we agree to pay the contract price mentioned in this Proposal, and according to the terms thereof. I/we acknowledge that before entering into this contract, I/we received a copy of the Notice to Owner which appears on the reverse side hereof. I/we have read and agree to the provisions contained on the front and reverse sides hereof, and in any attachments hereto, which are made a part hereof and are described as _____

_____.

ACCEPTED: _____
(Owner's Signature)   (Date)

_____
Owner's Name

_____
Street Address

City   State   Zip

Business Address   ( )   Business Phone No

> **Contractors are required by law to be licensed and regulated by the Contractors' State License Board. Any questions concerning a contractor may be referred to the Registrar, Contractors' State License Board, P.O. Box 26000, Sacramento, California 95826.**

If either the proposal and/or the acceptance of this Proposal and Contract is made at other than the premises at which Contractor or Owner normally carries on a business, then you, the Buyer, may cancel this transaction at any time prior to midnight of the third business day after the date of this transaction. See the attached Notice of Cancellation form (Wolcotts Form 560) for an explanation of this right.

The provision that Owner may cancel this transaction within three business days shall not apply to a contract in which Owner has initiated the Contract and which is executed in connection with the making of emergency repairs or services which are necessary for the immediate protection of persons or real or personal property, provided that Owner furnishes Contractor with a separate dated and signed personal statement describing the situation requiring immediate remedy and expressly acknowledging and waiving the right to cancel the sale within three business days (Wolcotts Form 570). IMPORTANT: SEE REVERSE SIDE FOR IMPORTANT INFORMATION © 1984 WOLCOTTS, INC

WOLCOTTS FORM 564—PROPOSAL AND CONTRACT FOR HOME IMPROVEMENT (padded)—Rev. 12-84   *See Form 564NHI for a Proposal and Contract NOT for Home Improvement (padded)
(Price class 4-2P)   (This form also available as a quad set - order Wolcotts Form 564Q)   or Form 564NHIQ for a Proposal and Contract NOT for Home Improvement (quad set)
Before you use this form, read it, fill in all blanks, and make whatever changes are appropriate and necessary to your particular transaction. Consult a lawyer if you doubt the form's fitness for your purpose and use. Wolcotts makes no representation or warranty, express or implied, with respect to the merchantability or fitness of this form for an intended use or purpose

Figure 4–2 (continued)

TERMS AND CONDITIONS (Continued)

1. The following terms and conditions apply to the payment schedule on the reverse side:

a. If the payment schedule contained in the contract provides for a downpayment to be paid to Contractor by Owner before the commencement of work, such downpayment shall not exceed One Thousand Dollars ($1,000) or 10% of the contract price, excluding finance charges, whichever is the lesser.

b. In no event shall the payment schedule provide for Contractor to receive, nor shall Contractor actually receive, payment in excess of 100% of the value of the work performed on the project at any time, excluding finance charges, except that Contractor may receive an initial downpayment authorized by condition (a), above.

c. A failure by Contractor without lawful excuse to substantially commence work within twenty (20) days of the approximate date specified in this Proposal and Contract when work will begin shall postpone the next succeeding payment to Contractor for that period of time equivalent to the time between when substantial commencement was to have occurred and when it did occur.

d. The terms and conditions set forth in sub-paragraphs (a), (b), and (c) above pertaining to the payment schedule shall not apply when the contract provides for Contractor to furnish a performance and payment bond, lien and completion bond, bond equivalent, or joint control approved by the Registrar of Contractors covering full performance and completion of the contract and such bonds or joint control is or are furnished by Contractor, or when the parties agree for full payment to be made upon or for a schedule of payments to commence after satisfactory completion of the project.

2. **WARNING:** a. Do not use this form if the owner is going to pay interest or any finance charge. A Home Improvement Contract with finance charges must comply both with the California Retail Installment Sales (Unruh) Act and the Federal Truth in Lending Act. The Federal Truth in Lending Act also applies if the contract price is payable in more than four installments even if there is no interest or finance charges. (Note: Progress payments are not installment payments.)

b. Do not use this form if this is a contract for construction of a swimming pool.

3. For your assistance the complete text of Sections 7151, 7151.2 and 7159 of the California Business and Professions Code are quoted below under the "Notice to Owner."

NOTICE TO OWNER

(Section 7018.5—Contractors License Law)

THE LAW REQUIRES THAT, BEFORE A LICENSED CONTRACTOR CAN ENTER INTO A CONTRACT WITH YOU FOR A WORK OF IMPROVEMENT ON YOUR PROPERTY, HE MUST GIVE YOU A COPY OF THIS NOTICE.

Under the California Mechanics' Lien Law any contractor, subcontractor, laborer, supplier or other person who helps to improve your property, but is not paid for his/her work or supplies, has a right to enforce a claim against your property. This means that after a court hearing, your property could be sold by a court officer and the proceeds of the sale used to satisfy the indebtedness. This can happen even if you have paid your contractor in full if the subcontractor, laborers or suppliers remain unpaid.

To preserve their right to file a claim or lien against your property, certain claimants such as subcontractors or material suppliers are required to provide you with a document entitled "Preliminary Notice." Original (or prime) contractors and laborers for wages do not have to provide this notice. A Preliminary Notice is not a lien against your property. Its purpose is to notify you of persons who may have a right to file a lien against your property if they are not paid. (Generally, the maximum time allowed for filing a claim or lien against your property is ninety [90] days after completion of your project).

TO INSURE EXTRA PROTECTION FOR YOURSELF AND YOUR PROPERTY, YOU MAY WISH TO TAKE ONE OR MORE OF THE FOLLOWING STEPS:

1. Require that your contractor supply you with a payment and performance bond (not a license bond), which provides that the bonding company will either complete the project or pay damages up to the amount of the bond. This payment and performance bond as well as a copy of the construction contract should be filed with the county recorder for your further protection.

2. Require that payments be made directly to subcontractors and material suppliers through a joint control. Any joint control agreement should include the addendum approved by the Registrar of Contractors.

3. Issue joint checks for payment, made out to both your contractor and subcontractors or material suppliers involved in the project. This will help to insure that all persons due payment are actually paid.

4. After making payment on any completed phase of the project, and before making any further payments, require your contractor to provide you with unconditional lien releases signed by each material supplier, subcontractor and laborer involved in that portion of the work for which payment was made. On projects involving improvements to a single family residence or a duplex owned by individuals, the persons signing these releases lose the right to file a claim against your property. In other types of construction this protection may still be important, but may not be as complete. TO PROTECT YOURSELF UNDER THIS OPTION YOU MUST BE CERTAIN THAT ALL MATERIAL SUPPLIERS, SUBCONTRACTORS AND LABORERS HAVE SIGNED.

CALIFORNIA BUSINESS AND PROFESSIONS CODE

§ 7151 Home improvement; home improvement goods or services; definitions

"Home improvement" means the repairing, remodeling, altering, converting, of modernizing of, or adding to, residential property and shall include, but not be limited to, the construction, erection, replacement, or improvement of driveways, swimming pools not subject to the provisions of Section 7167, terraces, patios, landscaping, fences, porches, garages, fallout shelters, basements, and other improvements of the structures or land which is adjacent to a dwelling house "Home improvement" shall also mean the installation of home improvement goods or the furnishing of home improvement services

For purposes of this chapter, "home improvement goods or services" means goods and services, as defined in Section 1689.5 of the Civil Code, which are bought in connection with the improvement of real property. Such home improvement goods and services include, but are not limited to carpeting, texture coating, fencing, air conditioning or heating equipment, and termite extermination Home improvement goods include goods which are to be so affixed to real property as to become a part of real property whether or not severable therefrom

§ 7152.2. Home improvement contract defined

"Home improvement contract" means an agreement, whether oral or written, or contained in one or more documents, between a contractor and an owner or between a contractor and a tenant, regardless of the number of residence or dwelling units contained in the building in which the tenant resides, if the work is to be performed in, to, or upon the residence or dwelling unit of such tenant, for the performance of a home improvement and includes all labor, services, and materials to be furnished and performed thereunder "Home improvement contract" also means an agreement, whether oral or written, or contained in one or more documents, between a salesman, whether or not he is a home improvement salesman, and (a) an owner or (b) a tenant, regardless of the number of residence or dwelling units contained in the building in which the tenant resides, which provides for the sale, installation, or furnishing of home improvement goods or services

§ 7159 Contract requirements; effect of noncompliance; violations

This section shall apply only to home improvement contracts, as defined in Section 7151.2, between a contractor, whether a general contractor or a specialty contractor, who is licensed or subject to be licensed pursuant to this chapter with regard to such transaction and who contracts with an owner or tenant for work upon a building or structure for proposed repairing, remodeling, altering, converting, or modernizing such building or structure and where the aggregate contract price specified in one or more improvement contracts, including all labor, services, and materials to be furnished by the contractor, exceeds five hundred dollars ($500).

Every home improvement contract and any changes in the contract subject to the provisions of this section shall be evidenced by a writing and shall be signed by all the parties to the contract thereto The writing shall contain the following:

(a) The name, address, and license number of the contractor, and the name and registration number of any salesman who solicited or negotiated the contract.

(b) The approximate dates when the work will begin and be substantially completed.

(c) A description of the work to be done and description of the materials to be used and the equipment to be used or installed and the agreed consideration for the work.

(d) If the payment schedule contained in the contract provides for a downpayment to be paid to the contractor by the owner or the tenant before the commencement of work, such downpayment shall not exceed one thousand dollars ($1,000) or 10 percent of the contract price, excluding finance charges, whichever is the lesser.

(e) A schedule of payments showing the amount of each payment as a sum in dollars and cents In no event shall the payment schedule provide for the contractor to receive, or shall the contractor actually receive, payments in excess of 100 percent of the value of the work performed on the project at any time, excluding finance charges, except that the contractor may receive an initial downpayment authorized by subdivision (d). A failure by the contractor without lawful excuse to substantially commence work within twenty (20) days of the approximate date specified in the contract when work will begin shall postpone the next succeeding payment to the contractor for that period of time equivalent to the time between when substantial commencement was to have occurred and when it did occur The schedule of payments shall be stated in dollars and cents, and shall be specifically referenced to the amount of work or services to be performed and to any materials and equipment to be supplied With respect to a contract which provides for a schedule of monthly payments to be made by the owner or tenant and for a schedule of payments to be disbursed to the contractor by a person or entity to whom the contractor intends to assign the right to receive the owner's or tenant's monthly payments, the payments referred to in this subdivision mean the payments to be disbursed by the assignee and not those payments to be made by the owner or tenant

(f) The requirements of subdivisions (d) and (e) pertaining to the payment schedule shall not apply when the contract provides for the contractor to furnish a performance and payment bond, lien and completion bond, bond equivalent, or joint control approved by the Registrar of Contractors covering full performance and completion of the contract and such bonds or joint control is or are furnished by the contractor, or when the parties agree for full payment to be made upon or for a schedule of payments to commence after satisfactory completion of the project The contract shall contain in close proximity to the signatures of the owner and contractor a notice in at least 10-point type stating that such owner or tenant has the right to require the contractor to have a performance and payment bond

(g) If the contract provides for a payment of a salesman's commission out of the contract price, such payment shall be made on a pro rata basis in proportion to the schedule of payments made to the contractor by the disbursing party in accordance with subdivision (e)

(h) The language of the notice required pursuant to Section 7018.5

(i) What constitutes substantial commencement of work pursuant to the contract

(j) A notice that failure by the contractor without lawful excuse to substantially commence work within twenty (20) days from the approximate date specified in the contract when work will begin is a violation of the Contractors License Law

(k) If the contract provides for a contractor to furnish joint control, the contractor shall not have any financial or other interest in such joint control

A failure by the contractor without lawful excuse to substantially commence work within twenty (20) days from the approximate date specified in the contract when work will begin is a violation of this section.

This section shall not be construed to prohibit the parties to a home improvement contract from agreeing to a contract or account subject to Chapter 1 (commencing with Section 1801) of Title 2 of Part 4 of Division 3 of the Civil Code.

The writing may also contain other matters agreed to by the parties to the contract

The writing shall be legible and shall be in such form as to clearly describe any other document which is to be incorporated into the contract, and before any work is done, the owner shall be furnished a copy of the written agreement, signed by the contractor.

For purposes of this section, the board shall, by regulation, determine what constitutes "without lawful excuse."

The provisions of this section are not exclusive and do not relieve the contractor or any contract subject to it from compliance with all other applicable provisions of law.

A violation of this section by a licensee, or a person subject to be licensed, under this chapter, his agent, or salesman is a misdemeanor punishable by a fine of not less than one hundred dollars ($100) nor more than five thousand dollars ($5,000) or by imprisonment in the county jail not exceeding one year, or by both such fine and imprisonment.

Figure 4-3

Sample Subcontract Agreement Form (Used by permission of Wolcotts, Inc.)

BUILDER'S SUB-CONTRACT AGREEMENT

This is a proposal to perform work at _____,

made this _____ day of _____, 19___, by _____,

hereinafter "Subcontractor," with principal office at _____:

to _____, hereinafter "Contractor,"

with principal office at _____.

Subcontractor proposes the following provisions:

_____ agree to furnish all materials and perform all labor necessary to complete the following as per plans and specifications:
(include job address): _____

_____

_____

All of the above materials to be the best of their respective kinds and all work to be completed in a substantial and workmanlike manner:

For the sum of _____ Dollars ($_____)
payable as follows:

_____

_____

_____

Any alteration or deviation from plans or specifications, whether involving extra cost of materials or labor or not, will be executed only upon written order for same, and will become an extra charge or credit when approved in writing by all parties concerned. It is further agreed that

_____ will carry all necessary compensation or liability insurance for the protection of all parties working on the building under the control of or in the employ of Subcontractor, also public liability insurance. The above proposal and contract becomes binding when

approved and accepted by Contractor. _____ further agrees to hold the Owner, Contractor and/or supervisor harmless from any and all Federal and State taxes allocable to the labor or material furnished and/or installed by Subcontractor.

This proposal is valid until _____. _____ agrees to begin work within
_____ days of written notice of approval and acceptance of this subcontract agreement by Contractor, and to continue said work diligently to completion, and if, in the opinion of Contractor, the job is not proceeding fast enough, Contractor may give Subcontractor notice in

writing, allowing him _____ (___ ___) hours in which to supply the necessary labor or material.

Should Subcontractor fail or refuse to comply with the written request, Contractor may order such labor and material as is necessary to complete the job and the cost of same shall be paid by Subcontractor, provided, however, Subcontractor may claim and receive benefit of any excuses for delay to which Contractor under his original contract with the Owner is entitled and to the same extent.

_____

_____

Contractors are required by law to be licensed and regulated by the Contractors' State License Board.
Any questions concerning a contractor may be referred to the Registrar of the Board,
Contractors' State License Board, P.O. Box 26000, Sacramento, CA 95826.

Respectfully submitted:

Subcontractor _____

License No. _____

Policy No. _____

By _____

Approved and accepted this ____ day of _____, 19__,

at _____, California

Contractor _____

License No. _____

By _____

Date	$	Received Payment
Date _____	$ _____	Received Payment _____
Date _____	$ _____	Received Payment _____
Date _____	$ _____	Received Payment _____
Date _____	$ _____	Received Payment _____
Date _____	$ _____	Received Payment _____
Date _____	$ _____	Received Payment _____

BUILDER'S SUB-CONTRACT AGREEMENT
WOLCOTTS FORM 566—Rev. 7-81

© 1981 WOLCOTTS, INC.

This standard form covers most usual problems in the field indicated. Before you sign, read it, fill in all blanks, and make changes proper to your transaction. Consult a lawyer if you doubt the form's fitness for your purpose.

Wolcotts forms can be purchased at most good office supply or stationery stores.

Figure 4–4

Addendum

The following addendum shall be including and become part of Proposal and Construction Subcontract agreement between _____ (Tradesman) _____, in the city of _____, State of _____.

1. (Tradesman) may make no assignment of any part of this agreement without the express written consent of the Owner/Builder.

2. (Tradesman) agrees that he will provide a written certificate of insurance, as proof of his coverage for worker's compensation and liability insurance, as a condition of this agreement. This written proof must be submitted to the Owner/Builder prior to the commencement of any work.

3. Owner/Builder reserves the right to reject the use of any and all building materials intended for use on this project which he, in his sole discretion, does not feel meets acceptable standards.

4. Owner/Builder is to be notified prior to enclosure of any walls so that he may conduct a visual inspection of the work performed. The Owner/Builder, should he choose to conduct said inspection, shall not cause a delay nor shall he interfere with the work progress of (the Tradesman).

5. Upon receipt of progress payment for materials, (the Tradesman) shall provide the Owner/Builder with signed "Unconditional Waiver and Release Upon Final Payment" forms from each and every material supplier to the project.

6. Upon receipt of the final progress payment, (the Tradesman) shall provide the Owner/Builder with an "Unconditional Waiver and Release Upon Final Payment" form signed by (the Tradesman) and all parties working on the project under (the Tradesman) control or in (his) employ.

7. Tradesman agrees that he shall have no authorization to perform additional work above and beyond what was originally agreed to without a written consent and authorization from the Owner/Builder.

8. Tradesman agrees to be available to complete the work on the dates scheduled and agreed to by both parties.

9. Tradesman agrees to provide his *first* and best crew to complete the designated work.

Reasons for including items are as follows: (1)to ensure that subcontractor does not hire another sub to do the work without your consent; (2) to ensure that subcontractor has workers' compensation and liability insurance to cover his workers and any other person(s) injured on the job (this will reduce your personal liability); (3) to maintain your own quality control over materials provided by subcontractor; (4) to maintain quality control over the project; (5) to avoid being liable to a material supplier because your subcontractor failed to pay for items that you already paid him for (see Figure 4–8); (6) to avoid liability toward the workers themselves (see Figure 4–8); (7) to avoid miscommunication (see Figure 4–9); (8) to insure availability on the scheduled dates; (9) to insure the use of his best crew.

---

be provided to you before the performance of any work. If a person is injured while working on your project and his employer, your subcontractor, is without coverage, you could be held liable for the injuries sustained. Make sure you review your insurance as well (see Chapter 2).

Another item that some people include is what I refer to as the "penalty" clause, which is basically designed to "punish" the tradesman for finishing the work beyond the completion date. It may take the form of something like this: "For every day that the work remains unfinished beyond the mutually agreed upon completion date, the (builder) agrees to reduce his fee by a rate of $100 per day."

In my view, this penalty clause is a mistake because it could ultimately harm you. If the tradesman were to fall behind schedule and was concerned that you would hold him to the deadline, he would, of course, rush the job, causing the quality of the work to deteriorate. The irony is that the job may suffer in ways you would not notice at first. If the subcontractor cuts corners, you may discover problems later on that will cost you far more than you would gain from a penalty clause. The tradesman's greatest incentive to finish your job on time is that final paycheck and the need to get on to the next paying job.

When you are establishing your ground rules and drawing your contracts, it is very important for everyone to understand that no final payments will be issued until a few conditions are met. I recommend that this final payment should represent not less than 15% of the entire cost. Don't let your subcontractor talk you into holding back less, since this amount may represent his profit. Let us discuss these all important conditions.

HOLD ON TO THAT LAST PAYMENT CHECK UNTIL . . .

You Are Completely Satisfied

Never, I repeat, never agree to release the final paycheck until the work is completed to your total satisfaction. This is not to say that even after a person has been paid in full, the subcontractor's sense of professionalism would not direct him to return and finish the job properly. It's just that it is simply human nature to perform better in anticipation of the reward (the money in this case) rather than after the reward has already been received.

Just consider how motivated you might be to work hard if your employer were to pay you in advance. Is it any great surprise that neither you nor anyone you know has an employer who does this? Completing the job to your satisfaction will assume a higher priority for the tradesman who anticipates, rather than already holds, his final payment.

You Have Obtained the Proper Lien Releases

This is another crucial reason not to be in a hurry to release that final payment. You will want to be absolutely sure that you have obtained the proper lien releases from every supplier (both material and labor) having anything to do with your project. Failure to do so may result in a lien against your property even if you have paid your subcontractor in full. Your sub could simply decide to walk away from his debt obligations to his suppliers and workers; he would, as a result, leave you holding the bag. Remember that you are ultimately responsible for seeing that everyone has been paid. Your best protection is to insist that *all* applicable parties sign these waivers.

Several waiver and release forms are available for different purposes. The sample forms included here (Figures 4–5, 4–6, 4–7, and 4–8) are used in California. Check with your local building department to determine which, if any, forms may be applicable in your state.

WATCH OUT FOR EXTRAS

We talked a little bit about "extras" in Chapter 2. You already know that they can cause you to go way over budget if you are not careful. One way to ensure that any changes to the original plans and contracting agreement are fully understood and agreed to by both parties in advance is to require completion of a "Change in Plans and Specifications" form (see Figure 4–9). You should insist that one of these forms be filled out before the subcontractor performs any "extra" work. Failure to do so leads to the potential for communication mix-ups. You may think you had agreed to one thing and the subcontractor will say that he thought you had agreed to something else. Completing one of these forms eliminates all doubt and avoids trouble down the road.

On one job, I had contracted a professional sewage system contractor to install a new septic tank for a house to accommodate the additional

Figure 4–5

Sample Conditional Waiver and Release upon Progress Payment Form

You would use this form when you have given your subcontractor or material supplier a progress payment check but the check has not yet cleared your bank. The lien release covering that particular phase of the project becomes effective when the check has cleared the bank. (Used by permission of Wolcotts, Inc.)

CONDITIONAL WAIVER AND RELEASE UPON PROGRESS PAYMENT
[California Civil Code §3262(d)(1)]

Upon receipt by the undersigned of a check from _____

(Maker of Check)

in the sum of $_____ payable to _____

(Amount of Check)   (Payee or Payees of Check)

and when the check has been properly endorsed and has been paid by the bank upon which it is drawn, this document shall become effective to release pro tanto* any mechanic's lien, stop notice

or bond right the undersigned has on the job of _____

(Owner)

located at _____ to the following extent.

(Job Description)

This release covers a progress payment for labor, services, equipment or material furnished to

_____ through _____

(Your Customer)   (Date)

only and does not cover any retention or items furnished after said date. Before any recipient of this document relies on it, said party should verify evidence of payment to the undersigned.

Dated: _____   _____

(Company Name)

By _____

(Title)

*For so much; for as much as may be; as far as it goes.

NOTE: This form of release complies with the requirements of Civil Code Section 3262(d)(1). It is to be used by a party who applies for a progress payment when the progress payment check has not yet cleared the bank. This release only becomes effective when the check, properly endorsed, has cleared the bank.

USE REVERSE SIDE AS RELEASE FOR INDIVIDUALS PERFORMING LABOR FOR WAGES

WOLCOTTS FORM 3262.1—CONDITIONAL WAIVER AND RELEASE UPON PROGRESS PAYMENT—Rev. 1-85   © 1985 WOLCOTTS, INC.

(price class 7-2)

Wolcotts forms can be purchased at most good office supply or stationery stores.

Figure 4–6

Sample Unconditional Waiver and Release upon Progress Payment Form
Use this form when your subcontractor or material supplier has acknowledged receipt of your progress payment and grants the waiver. (Used by permission of Wolcotts, Inc.)

UNCONDITIONAL WAIVER AND RELEASE UPON PROGRESS PAYMENT
[California Civil Code §3262(d)(2)]

The undersigned has been paid and has received a progress payment in the sum of $_____

for labor, services, equipment or material furnished to _____
(Your Customer)

on the job of _____ located at _____
(Owner)   (Job Description)
_____ and does hereby release pro tanto* any mechanic's lien, stop notice, or bond right that the undersigned has on the above referenced job to the following extent. This release covers a

progress payment for labor, services, equipment or material furnished to _____
(Your Customer)
_____ through _____ only and does not cover any retention
(Date)

or items furnished after that date.

Dated: _____   _____
                                                           (Company Name)

                                    By _____
                                                           (Title)

NOTICE TO PERSONS SIGNING THIS WAIVER: THIS DOCUMENT WAIVES RIGHTS UNCONDITIONALLY AND STATES THAT YOU HAVE BEEN PAID FOR GIVING UP THOSE RIGHTS. THIS DOCUMENT IS ENFORCEABLE AGAINST YOU IF YOU SIGN IT, EVEN IF YOU HAVE NOT BEEN PAID. IF YOU HAVE NOT BEEN PAID, USE A CONDITIONAL RELEASE FORM.

*For so much; for as much as may be; as far as it goes.

NOTE: This form of release complies with the requirements of Civil Code Section 3262(d)(2). It is to be used to release claims to the extent that a progress payment has actually been received by the releasing party.

USE REVERSE SIDE AS RELEASE FOR INDIVIDUALS PERFORMING LABOR FOR WAGES

Wolcotts forms can be purchased in most good office supply or stationery stores.

Figure 4–7

Sample Conditional Waiver and Release upon Final Payment Form

For use when your supplier has acknowledged receipt of your final check, but it has not as yet cleared your bank. The waiver and release becomes effective when the funds clear your bank. (Used by permission of Wolcotts, Inc.)

CONDITIONAL WAIVER AND RELEASE UPON FINAL PAYMENT
[California Civil Code §3262(d)(3)]

Upon receipt by the undersigned of a check from _____
(Maker of Check)
in the sum of $_____ payable to _____
(Amount of Check)   (Payee or Payees of Check)
and when the check has been properly endorsed and has been paid by the bank upon which it is drawn, this document shall become effective to release any mechanic's lien, stop notice, or bond

right the undersigned has on the job of _____
(Owner)
located at _____.
(Job Description)
This release covers the final payment to the undersigned for all labor, services, equipment or material furnished on the job, except for disputed claims for additional work in the amount of

$_____. Before any recipient of this document relies on it, the party should verify evidence of payment to the undersigned.

Dated: _____   _____
(Company Name)

By _____
(Title)

NOTE: This form of release complies with the requirements of Civil Code Section 3262(d)(3). It is not effective until the check that constitutes final payment has been properly endorsed, and has cleared the bank.

USE REVERSE SIDE AS RELEASE FOR INDIVIDUALS PERFORMING LABOR FOR WAGES

WOLCOTTS FORM 3262 3—CONDITIONAL WAIVER AND RELEASE UPON FINAL PAYMENT—Rev 1-85
(price class 7-2)   1985 WOLCOTTS INC

Wolcotts forms can be purchased at most good office supply or stationery stores.

Figure 4–8

Sample Unconditional Waiver and Release upon Final Payment Form

This form is used when your supplier has acknowledged receipt of payment and effectively relinquishes all rights to enforce a lien against your property. (Used by permission of Wolcotts, Inc.)

UNCONDITIONAL WAIVER AND RELEASE UPON FINAL PAYMENT
[California Civil Code §3262(d)(4)]

The undersigned has been paid in full for all labor, services, equipment or material furnished

to _____ on the job of _____
          (Your Customer)   (Owner)

_____ located at _____
                                                              (Job Description)

and does hereby waive and release any right to a mechanic's lien, stop notice, or any right against a

labor and material bond on the job, except for disputed claims for extra work in the amount of

$_____.

Dated: _____   _____
                                                                        (Company Name)

                                                    By _____
                                                                        (Title)

NOTICE TO PERSONS SIGNING THIS WAIVER: THIS DOCUMENT WAIVES RIGHTS UNCONDITIONALLY AND STATES THAT YOU HAVE BEEN PAID FOR GIVING UP THOSE RIGHTS. THIS DOCUMENT IS ENFORCEABLE AGAINST YOU IF YOU SIGN IT, EVEN IF YOU HAVE NOT BEEN PAID. IF YOU HAVE NOT BEEN PAID, USE A CONDITIONAL RELEASE FORM.

NOTE: This form of release complies with the requirements of Civil Code Section 3262(d)(4).

USE REVERSE SIDE AS RELEASE FOR INDIVIDUALS PERFORMING LABOR FOR WAGES

WOLCOTTS FORM 3262.4—UNCONDITIONAL WAIVER AND RELEASE UPON FINAL PAYMENT   Rev. 1-85
(price class 7-2)   1985 WOLCOTTS INC

Wolcotts forms can be purchased at most good office supply or stationery stores.

Figure 4–8A

Common Backside to Figures 4–5, 4–6, 4–7, and 4–8

THE UNDERDESIGNED HAVE PERFORMED LABOR FOR WAGES ON THE PROJECT DESCRIBED ON FACE OF FORM AND HAVE BEEN PAID IN FULL TO DATE

(Signature Of Individual Performing Labor For Wages)	(Date)	(Signature Of Individual Performing Labor For Wages)	(Date)
(Signature Of Individual Performing Labor For Wages)	(Date)	(Signature Of Individual Performing Labor For Wages)	(Date)
(Signature Of Individual Performing Labor For Wages)	(Date)	(Signature Of Individual Performing Labor For Wages)	(Date)
(Signature Of Individual Performing Labor For Wages)	(Date)	(Signature Of Individual Performing Labor For Wages)	(Date)
(Signature Of Individual Performing Labor For Wages)	(Date)	(Signature Of Individual Performing Labor For Wages)	(Date)
(Signature Of Individual Performing Labor For Wages)	(Date)	(Signature Of Individual Performing Labor For Wages)	(Date)
(Signature Of Individual Performing Labor For Wages)	(Date)	(Signature Of Individual Performing Labor For Wages)	(Date)
(Signature Of Individual Performing Labor For Wages)	(Date)	(Signature Of Individual Performing Labor For Wages)	(Date)
(Signature Of Individual Performing Labor For Wages)	(Date)	(Signature Of Individual Performing Labor For Wages)	(Date)
(Signature Of Individual Performing Labor For Wages)	(Date)	(Signature Of Individual Performing Labor For Wages)	(Date)
(Signature Of Individual Performing Labor For Wages)	(Date)	(Signature Of Individual Performing Labor For Wages)	(Date)

BE SURE TO COMPLETE OTHER SIDE

Figure 4–9

Sample Change in Plans and Specifications Form
(Used by permission of Wolcotts, Inc.)

CHANGE IN PLANS AND SPECIFICATIONS

————◄►————

Date _____

THE UNDERSIGNED HEREBY AUTHORIZE__ _____

to make the following change__ from the work as originally set forth in the plans and specifications for

that construction contract dated _____:

_____

_____

_____

_____

_____ ,

for which an ADDITION/DEDUCTION of $_____ is made FROM/TO the contract price.

_____

Signed _____

WOLCOTTS FORM 572—CHANGE IN PLANS AND SPECIFICATIONS—Rev. 5-83   © 1983 WOLCOTTS, INC.
(price class 7-1)

bathrooms that were being added. I had already obtained my three estimates, and this contractor's price fell in the middle. He was a professional, was very well regarded in the community, and I liked him.

When I had first contacted him, I had told the sewage contractor that his estimate should not include connecting his line to the old system as new plumbing was planned. Things changed, and the plan to install a new line from the house was scrapped. Since his was the first bid I had obtained and I later changed my mind about the new line, I informed the subsequent two bidders that they were to make the connection. I promptly forgot that I had told the first bidder something other than what I told the other two. (*Note:* Always be sure that all your bidders compete based on the same specifications and related information.)

A month and a half later when the contractor finally did do the work, I told him to connect to the house. He never questioned me nor did he remind me that his original bid did not include the connection to the house. Neither of us questioned the other about what we had agreed to in our original discussions.

When he presented the final bill, I was shocked to discover that he had added $150 to the cost for the connection, which required about five extra feet of pipe and one connector. Fortunately, he was an honorable man and agreed that there had probably been some miscommunication and was willing to share the responsibility. We agreed to split the increased cost, and I ended up paying only $75 for the connection. From then on, I have insisted on an agreement that requires all "extras" to be approved in writing and in advance of the commencement of the work.

Now we have established some ground rules that everyone can live with. I'm sure that you can think of others, but remember, it is not in your best interest to overwhelm each other with all possible contingencies. It is essential to maintain an open mind and some flexibility and to keep the lines of communication open between you and your workers. You can work together in resolving problems as long as all parties have a general understanding of what is expected of them.

REVIEW

Do's

- Do hire professionals.

- Do check references and ask the right questions.

- Do obtain at least three bids.
- Do use your common sense when negotiating for costs.
- Do establish ground rules.
- Do insist that your subcontractors provide proof of insurance.
- Do attach an addendum to a tradesman's form contract.
- Do obtain lien releases from *all* suppliers.
- Do require your written authorization in advance on all "extras."
- Do maintain some flexibility.

Don'ts

- Don't hire someone who comes to you.
- Don't always take the middle or lowest bid.
- Don't insert a penalty clause.
- Don't release the final payment until you are satisfied.
- Don't release the final payment without all lien releases.

Let the Project Begin

Up until this point we have gone through the preplanning stages. You have developed your "family plan" and have thought about what you want the final project to look like. The draftsman or architect has drawn up the finished plans. These blueprints have been approved by the local city or county building department. The subcontractors or tradesmen have been contracted. Financing is in place. You are now ready to begin the project. Right? Well almost. You will need a few things before you begin. We'll start with the purchase of some materials.

You should already have estimated the costs for materials you will need based on the discussion in Chapter 2. I have already mentioned that as the "owner-builder" and "manager" of your project, you will want to consider purchasing most of your materials yourself. Some builders and tradesmen may argue that they can get better deals because they are entitled to a contractor's discount and because they purchase in greater volume. You may want to have them try and prove it. Who is to say that you can't get the same good deals yourself?

If you prefer, ask your tradesmen to provide you with prices for the materials you will need. Just be certain that they break out the material prices to you separately from the costs for performing the work. That way you can be sure that you are comparing "apples with apples" when you obtain your own price. Don't forget that the tradesman would be using his own time to place the order and to arrange for delivery. In most, but not all cases, they would want to be compensated for their time and they would do this by "marking up" the cost of the materials to you. What, in your view, is a "fair" markup? It is up to you to make this determination based on your own price-shopping efforts.

Once a tradesman gives you his materials price, shop and compare on your own to see if he is indeed less expensive. I would be willing to bet that not only can you obtain the materials for less but you can have better control over the quality of what you receive. Remember, as discussed in Chapter 1, your time = dollars saved. If you want to save a great deal of money, you must become the person responsible for shopping the best prices on materials. This is going to take some time but you will have the satisfaction of knowing that you are searching out the best deals. Your personal challenge should always be to beat by substantial margins the prices given for estimating purposes. It really is fun and profitable to see how well you can ultimately do.

If you feel that shopping for materials and less expensive labor costs is beneath you and that your time is far too valuable to be wasted, examine just how great the resultant savings can be. The following example describes the typical results of this kind of effort.

When we had to arrange for the installation of the closet organizers for a new addition, we were faced with a few options. We needed a total of four closet organizers. As you probably already know, these organizers are made of lumber and/or rubber-coated wire and are designed to maximize closet space by compartmentalizing; that is, separate racks for shoes, sweaters, shirts, long jackets and pants, and so on.

Since they were to be made out of lumber, the first option was to pay a finish carpenter to design and build them one at a time. All four closets were of different design and length (15', 12', 8', 5'). We estimated that having the material purchased by the finish carpenter, on a piecemeal basis, would have cost us nearly $1,900. And the estimated cost for the carpenter's time would have added another $3,200 to the cost of completing the closets.

We called a local company that specializes in closet organizer construction and installation to get another price. They told us that it would cost between $800 and $1,500 for an average-sized closet (average being about 6′ in length by about 8′ in height). We had the equivalent of more than six average-sized closets to be made. Using the cheapest price available, $800 per closet, the cost would have exceeded $4,800 for all four closets.

Instead of paying $4,800 for the closet organizers, we achieved a first-class job for less than $1,200 for *all* four closets, saving more than $3,600 on the cost. It took about 6 hours of our personal time. We had to find some workers who had all the experience of building the closets but without the same overhead expenses to drive up their costs. Our subcontractors often employed workers who exhibited great skills but were happy to work for an hourly wage. They were pleased to do the job while avoiding the responsibilities and expenses of being an employer because they liked, from time to time, to "moonlight" for a little extra pay. We simply employed a few of these people to work directly for us *after* their regular work hours and on weekends.

I should caution you that I am not encouraging you simply to hire someone else's employees. Nothing could be less scrupulous than to take money out of a subcontractor's pocket in this way. Hiring their people directly should only be considered with the employer's full knowledge and consent. In this particular case, we had brought the employer in to complete another task and he was not the least bit interested in building the closet organizers. We simply asked him if it was okay to have his people work directly for us on the side. Since he had no problem with this arrangement, it was a winning situation all the way around.

In this situation, I prefer to have the workers give us a flat price rather than paying them by the hour. Since they would be working after "peak energy" hours, we wanted to be sure to have a firm price regardless of how long they took to do the job. They agreed to $650 for the whole project. A fair price to be sure and still more than they were accustomed to.

These workers even assisted us in locating and picking up the materials. I went into the wholesale lumber supply company, told the manager that I was an owner-builder, and asked if he would please offer me a builder's discount. He enthusiastically agreed, and I walked out with all materials necessary to complete the task. The total cost for materials was $465.

All you have to do to save money this way is be willing to spend a little time asking around and diligently searching for the right people. The amount of money you can save will astound you.

LET'S SHOP UNTIL WE DROP

Later in this chapter I will discuss in greater detail how to negotiate the best deals on materials. First, however, I would like to better prepare you for your shopping expedition with some simple suggestions.

Shopping for materials is time-consuming work and you are going to want to make the most of it. You will need detailed lists to fulfill your building material purchases, as some of these needed items may be unfamiliar to you.

I would recommend that you begin by preparing a list for each portion of the project. Remember now, your tradesmen should tell you everything they will need. Just because they are not procuring the items does not mean they don't have to specify materials. Be sure to pin them down to as many things as they can think of before you go shopping. You will have better negotiating power with the supplier if you can present a large list on your initial visit rather than going back several times and piecemealing it.

List each phase of the project on its own separate sheet of paper. One of your lists may look something like this:

Electrical Supply List

	Quantity	Cost
_____ Plugs/plates	_____	_____
_____ Single pole switches/plates	_____	_____
_____ 3-way switches/plates	_____	_____
_____ 12 Gauge wire or romex (in feet)	_____	_____
_____ Recessed light housing units	_____	_____
_____ Light boxes	_____	_____
_____ Single light switch/plug boxes	_____	_____
_____ Double light switch/plug boxes	_____	_____
_____ Junction boxes	_____	_____

	Quantity	Cost
_____ Yellow wire nuts (boxes)	_____	_____
_____ Red wire nuts (boxes)	_____	_____
_____ Subpanel (if necessary—specify type)	_____	_____
_____ Circuit breakers (specify size & type)	_____	_____

At first you may not know what each of the things on your list is used for. By all means, do ask your tradesman to fill you in on an item's use and have him explain the proper terminology. Understand, however, that it is not his job to teach you everything he knows. Your local library or bookstore stocks numerous fine books that provide valuable information on the terms for and uses of a great many building products. You will want to be somewhat knowledgeable so that you can sound intelligent when you go in to buy the items on your list.

It is also up to you to arrange for the materials to be there when your tradesmen need them. This makes proper scheduling essential. The last thing you want is for your framing contractor to be standing there with nothing to nail. If he has to stop what he is doing to go and buy something, you will lose time and money. I will discuss scheduling in greater detail later in this chapter.

CONGRATULATIONS! YOU'VE JUST BECOME A BUSINESS

In Chapter 1, I recommended using the "Business to Business" yellow pages when trying to find a draftsman. I also mentioned that this tool would be a valuable source for suppliers. Some of you may be thinking that the "Business to Business" yellow pages cater specifically to those businesses entitled to purchase wholesale or those that have obtained a resale license, but you should begin to think of yourself *as* a business. You have every right to buy wholesale too. If it is your intention to act as the "owner-builder" or "general contractor" on your particular project, why shouldn't you enjoy the same benefits that other professionals in the field do?

From this moment forward, you should act in your negotiations with suppliers as if you do this for a living. You can specifically say, if you are asked by wholesale suppliers, that you are the contractor on the job. This is not dishonest nor deceptive. After all, you have made yourself responsible for overseeing the work and hiring the subcontractors. You *are* the contractor-builder and you should never shy away from being treated as one.

I have never had my money refused by a wholesale supplier. Your cash is just as good as the next person's and, even though they may not want to admit it, wholesalers will deal with the general public. The problem for them arises when they are blatant about it, making them lose credibility with their regular professional clientele from whom they receive most of their business. For this reason, you should avoid wearing a business suit when you visit a supplier catering to the wholesale building trade and try to pass yourself off as a contractor. Even though by definition you are, you should dress in the same style as those around you so you do not look out of place. Just look and act as if you belong and you will have no problem buying wholesale.

Often wholesale suppliers will ask you if your purchase is for resale. What they want to know is if you intend, in turn, to sell this product to your customer, the ultimate end user. They must know this to determine whether to charge you sales tax on the purchased product. The rules may vary from state to state, but in California, if you had a resale license it would be your responsibility to collect the sales tax from the person to whom you sell something. Your patron would be what is known as the "end user." In this case, if you provided the wholesaler with a copy of your resale number and completed a resale card, he would not have to charge you sales tax. Since you will be the end user, you should always tell the wholesalers that your purchase is not for resale and have them charge you the applicable sales tax.

Even if you should find yourself dealing with proprietors who cater to the general public rather than wholesale to the trade, you should always ask if they offer a builder's discount. If they do, this could amount to 10% to 20% off the cost of your supplies. If not, you have not lost anything. Just continue in your search until you find a merchant who will give the discount. Remember that when you are dealing with suppliers, *everything* is negotiable.

You may have heard it said that we are the only country in the world whose people do not bargain. In this country, many people expect that just because a price is printed on a little tag attached to a product or on a piece of paper somewhere that it is positively nonnegotiable. You'll discover that this is not always the case.

People bargain all the time on the price of an automobile. Have you ever known anyone to pay sticker price for their car? What about a house?

Has anyone ever said, "Gee honey, we really did like that house but it's printed right here in black and white, $159,995 is the price. Do you think we should stretch ourselves and just tell the realtor we'll take it, or should we look for one with a price tag more in line with our budget of $150,000?" Some people still do pay the "printed" price on big-ticket items, but these people are the exception rather than the rule.

If a supplier were to put out a sign that read "We offer a discount to everyone who asks," of course many people would be tempted to ask for the discount. Why in the world would a merchant want to advertise that wares will be discounted if most people are willing to pay full price? You must ask for that discount. Don't be shy, just ask to speak to the manager or owner and perhaps explain that you will be buying a lot of building materials over the next several months and want to know if the store would be willing to offer a discount. If the manager asks how much of a discount you would like, for example, try 20%. If the manager says that is impossible but that he could offer 10%, be sure to say thank you, but ask for 15% and see what the reply is. You may be surprised when you get an agreement. It probably will be to the store's advantage to attract your volume business. Just remember to reward the consideration by returning to that store for future purchases. You win. The merchant wins. Everybody is happy, and you are well on your way to remodeling at wholesale.

By now you should have developed at least a sense of the type of materials shopper you must become. No, it is not easy and, yes, it is time consuming; but it is also certainly challenging and rewarding. You become a kind of detective, following down leads and using the resources available to you in seeking out the very best prices. How much money you actually save is entirely up to you, as you will likely save in direct proportion to the effort you put forth. If you planned properly, you should reduce your costs significantly, and your savings will more than compensate you for the time required to complete the task. Have some fun with your shopping! What you've got to lose is nothing. It is the savings you will gain that are important.

THE KEY TO YOUR SUCCESS AS A REMODELER: SCHEDULING

We talked a bit about scheduling back in Chapter 2. In that chapter, we examined it in relation to the order in which we gathered our estimates. By obtaining costs for the various phases in their proper order, you should have at least begun to understand which phase follows another. You may want to take a moment to review that chapter before continuing. It is very important to understand good management and scheduling techniques once your project gets underway.

Perhaps the most difficult function of being your project's "owner-builder" or "manager," if you decide to undertake that role, is in understanding how to properly schedule and manage your workers. How well you do will depend on how organized you are. When contemplating your role, try to remember these "Six P's": *P*roper *P*lanning *P*revents *P*itifully *P*oor *P*erformance. If you are poorly organized and allow your workers to sit around waiting for materials because you didn't order them in a timely fashion, you have not done your job. It is up to you to be sure that none of your subs ever has to be held up because you failed to plan ahead. You must also see to it that one tradesman is properly followed or overlapped by the next in an orderly fashion.

You certainly wouldn't want your painters to end up waiting for your finish carpenter to complete the installation of the crown molding and baseboards. What if your tilelayer threatened to undertake another six-week job before yours because your drywall subcontractor was late in finishing the bathrooms? These are just some of the horrors that can await you unless you are properly prepared.

Scheduling your subcontractors would be easy if all you had to do was call them in when you had completed each preceding phase of the project. Unfortunately for you, your subcontractors will undoubtedly have other jobs lined up and other commitments to fulfill. They are probably not standing by the phone waiting for your call informing them of your readiness to begin. You have to know *exactly* when they will be needed and have them lined up and committed to go well in advance. To do this, you're going to need a schedule and it should be in writing.

Developing a written schedule will help you in two ways. First, it will force you to focus on your responsibilities as the project manager. And second, it will assist you in coordinating and managing the responsibilities of your various subcontractors. Assembling the schedule prior to commencing the project leaves less room for confusion later on when time begins to equal money. For this exercise, follow along with the sample Home Remodeling Schedule shown in Figure 5–1.

Using the example from Chapter 2, we will assume that you will be adding a new wing to your existing home, which will be made up of a master suite (including bathroom) and a family room complete with wet bar and another half bathroom. The addition will measure 760 square feet.

Figure 5–1

Home Remodeling Schedule

	JANUARY	FEBRUARY	MARCH	APRIL	MAY	JUNE
1		Framing Continues	Rough Plumbing Continues	Roof Continues	Taping & Compound Continues	Painting Continues
2						
3					Tile Delivered	OPEN
4						Shower Door Del. & Installed
5			Masonry-Fireplace			Mirrors Installed
6					Bathroom Cab. Del.	Finish Heating & A.C. Registers & Testing
7				All Doors & Windows Delivered		OPEN
8	#1 Trash Bin Delivered			Exterior Doors & Windows Installed	Cabinets Installed	#2 Trash Bin Delivered
9	Demolition					Old Driveway Demolished & Removed
10						
11			Rough Heating & A.C.		OPEN	
12					Tile Work Begins	
13		Remove Debris				#3 Trash Bin Delivered
14	Excavating			OPEN		Cleanup
15			Rough Electrical	OPEN/Insulation Delivered	Int. Doors Installed	
16				Insulation Installed		
17					Wood Mantel & Finish Carp.	
18	Form Foundation			OPEN/Lap Material Delivered	Wood Flooring Delivered	New Driveway & Steps Installed
19				Wood Lap Siding Work Begins	Floor Installed	
20	Foundation Form Inspection					
21	Pour Concrete For Foundation					New Trees & Bushes Del.
22						
23				OPEN/Drywall Delivered		OPEN
24				Drywall Installed	Finish Electrical	
25	Septic Tank in	OPEN				
26		OPEN	OPEN			
27	Framing Lumber Delivered	Rough Plumbing	Rough Inspection	OPEN		Landscaping
28	Framing Begins		OPEN	Drywall Nailing Inspection	Painting	
29			Roof Flashing Sheet Metal	Taping & Joint Compound Application		Final Inspection
30						Project Complete
31			Roof Installation Begins			

Your plans have already passed through the approval process, and all your applicable building permits have been drawn. In talking to the subcontractors with whom you have entered into contractual arrangements, each has agreed to be available during the times that you will specify as soon as your schedule is prepared. Since you are planning so far in advance, you should have priority over other jobs that they may agree to undertake.

As a side note here, you will want to be sure that your subcontractor has promised you his "A-Team," or best crew, to be available for work on your project. Sometimes subcontractors will hire secondary, part-time crews when the volume of their work warrants it. Make sure that the best crew will be available for your project when needed. You certainly don't want to be paying for the A-Team and only getting the "Second String" because the best crew is held up on another job. This arrangement should be clearly spelled out in your contractual agreements (see Chapter 4, Figure 4–4).

You are now ready to begin preparing your schedule. As you can see from Figure 5–1, the starting date is January 9. Note that I have made allowances in this sample schedule for additional time to cover weekends and holidays, and you should remember to do the same. You should make arrangements for your first trash bin to be delivered the day before demolition begins. Let us assume that you have chosen to save some money by hiring your own labor crew and having them operate under your supervision. You have estimated that it will take your crew about two and a half days to complete the demolition portion of your project. To protect yourself, however, you double the amount of time you believe would be necessary to complete the task.

Following the demolition phase, some of your labor force will begin the excavation for the foundation while you retain a few workers to continue with the demolition cleanup phase (Remove Debris). You then arrange with your foundation subcontractor to commence with the formwork on January 18, in preparation for the pouring of the concrete. He informs you that he will need two days to form the foundation and only one day to pour the concrete.

Remember that you will need to call for an inspection of the foundation forms prior to pouring any concrete, so allow a full day for the inspector to arrive and approve your forms (see Chapter 1). You will also need to allow some time for the concrete to cure properly. For this you should plan on just about a week. During that time, you can schedule your septic tank subcontractor to come in and install the new tank.

You have made arrangements for all of your framing lumber and rough hardware to be delivered January 27 in preparation for the framing that is to begin the following day. The framer whom you have contracted has estimated that you can expect that portion of the project to take just under four weeks for completion. You leave a couple of open days—February 25 and 26—just in case the job runs beyond its scheduled completion date. Even if the framer were to run beyond those extra days, that work should not interfere with the plumber whom you have scheduled to begin on February 27.

While your rough plumbing is underway, you anticipate no conflict in having your masonry subcontractor begin work on the family room fireplace. Since he was, in fact, able to provide you with a better price on the brick than you could obtain, he will make his own arrangements for the delivery of all materials. You then schedule your masonry subcontractor from March 2 until March 10.

You can see here how your project schedule begins to take shape. You just have to be aware that it is not as simple as scheduling one tradesman after another. There will be times when you will have to schedule more than one phase during the same time period. Just be sure that you don't have one group of workers interfering with the progress of another.

You arrange for your heating and air-conditioning subcontractor to begin installing the plenum and returns for service to the new area on March 11. He needs about two and a half days to complete this rough phase. Since the electrical subcontractor will not interfere with the rough heating and air-conditioning work, you schedule the two phases to overlap. The rough electrical work begins March 12 and continues until March 25. If an extra day is required, you have scheduled March 26 as an open date and tentatively plan to call for the rough inspection on March 27. Keep in mind that you don't have to make arrangements for that rough inspection until at least a couple of days beforehand, so you have some latitude there if you need it (see Chapter 1).

The roof flashing/rough sheet metal work is scheduled to begin March 29. Your sheet metal subcontractor says it will take about a day and a half to do this job.

Immediately following this phase, the installation of your roof begins March 31 and continues through April 7. On or around the final day of the roof work, you arrange for the delivery of your new doors and windows. Installation for the exterior doors and windows is scheduled to begin April 8. The work is expected to take six days, but you leave a couple of days open just in case.

You expect to begin installing the insulation yourself on April 16 and plan to have the material delivered the day before. You're really not sure how long it will take you to do the work but estimate two days. Then, just to be safe, you leave yourself an extra day open before the exterior siding work is scheduled to begin.

It is a good idea to wait to begin the installation of the drywall until the work on the exterior has been completed. With all the nailing necessary to install the wood lap siding, you don't want to have to redo any of the interior drywall due to jarring or settling. For this reason your schedule does not overlap these two phases. You will make arrangements for the drywall material to be delivered April 23 and for your subcontractor to begin work the following day.

As you know from the discussion in Chapter 1, you will be required to arrange for an inspection of the "nailing" of your drywall. Your building department just wants to be sure that the drywall boards are adequately supported with nails and screws and that the boards will not fall down. This inspection will be tentatively scheduled for April 28 with the taping and the joint compound application phase to commence the following day. This work will continue until May 7. While it is underway, you will be expecting delivery of your ceramic tile and your bathroom cabinets.

Immediately following the completion of your drywall work, you have scheduled your finish carpenter to begin work on the installation of your bathroom cabinets. This will be followed by the commencement of your tile work on May 12. While this work is continuing, you have your finish carpenter follow the cabinetwork with the installation of the interior doors, wood mantel work, and the hardwood floors in your family room. You also schedule yourself to plan on spending your vacation completing the finish electrical work from May 21 through May 27. Your painting subcontractor will just be returning from vacation and will begin work on your project May 25 and continue until June 2.

Beginning with your planned date of June 4 to have the shower door delivered and installed, you begin a busy week of finish work. June 5 brings the installation of the bathroom mirrors followed by the return of your heating and air-conditioning subcontractor the following day. He will need the day to install your registers and thermostat and to test your new temperature control system.

On June 8, you have your second trash bin delivered. This bin, however, is smaller and is designed to carry only a certain weight of rock, or cement or, in this case, your old blacktop driveway. You're not sure if one bin will be sufficient to contain the remnants of your old driveway. If necessary, you are prepared to have the trash removal company dump one load and then return the bin to your job site. You already budgeted for this contingency when you estimated your costs (see Chapter 2).

The following day, you will plan to have your labor force break up your old driveway and load the pieces into the bin. You have estimated that it will take two workers a total of four days to complete the work. You then have scheduled these laborers to begin the final cleanup effort in preparation of the installation of your new concrete driveway. Trash bin 3 (or 4) will be scheduled for delivery on June 13.

June 18 brings the scheduled arrival of your driveway subcontractor. Since all the forming and the pouring of the concrete will be done by this sub, he has contractually agreed to pull the required permit and arrange for the inspection. This subcontractor has informed you that the job will require at least five days. During this time, you expect to have some new trees and bushes delivered in preparation for some landscaping work. This phase will commence immediately upon completion and curing of the new driveway.

By the end of June, you will have finally reached the completion of your project and be ready to call for the final inspection.

Once you have a rough schedule, ask yourself if you feel comfortable with the format. You can see why it is so important to develop and maintain such a written schedule, and to write your initial schedule in pencil. You can certainly expect to have to deal with some alterations in the planned schedule. Some juggling of the scheduled dates and your workers will become necessary. No matter how carefully you plan ahead, some delay problems are bound to arise.

Can you think of any problems that would cause a delay in your project? Consider the weather, illness, and other reasons, such as the dreaded truck breakdown epidemic, that might cause your subcontractors to become "no shows."

TRUCK BREAKDOWNS ARE EPIDEMIC WITH TRADESMEN

I've heard many excuses why some tradesmen did not show up when they were supposed to. These are some of the most common:

"Oh, was I supposed to come over today? I thought that we agreed to start tomorrow. Well, I guess we just got our signals crossed. Ha, Ha."

"You're not going to believe this but 'they' broke into my truck and stole most of my good tools. Well, of course I had to file a police report and talk with all those insurance people. Anyway, I should be there at your place 'bright and early' (which really means noon) tomorrow (which may really mean the day after tomorrow)."

"I'm sorry I'm running late but I'm having a problem with my truck." To which I would reply: "Well what sort of problem is it?" And they would say: "Gee, I'm not really sure. It must be something in the transmission." So I would say: "Do you have any idea what time you will have it fixed?" Their reply would almost always follow this pattern: "I . . . I really don't know for sure. I've got a guy who is supposed to come over and take a look at it, but he really couldn't tell me for sure what time that would be. Do . . . do you want me to just come tomorrow instead? I'm sure that I can get it fixed sometime today."

Of course I am having a little fun here. It is certainly not my intention here to label all tradesmen as flaky or unreliable. Nothing could be further from the truth. All the subs I have worked with have worked very hard when they had to. But, like most of us, tradesmen can slip up from time to time, so it's important to exercise patience when dealing with them. Your role as the "general contractor" or "manager" on your project should be to provide leadership tempered with a certain degree of tolerance for the foibles of those who work with you.

It is important to keep in mind, however, that regardless of your tolerance level in dealing with schedule delays caused by your workers, these delays will wreak havoc on your prepared schedule. To minimize the damage caused by delays, make sure that you maintain steady and regular contact with your various subcontractors. Keeping them informed of your progress, or should I say your lack of it, will go a long way toward garnering flexibility on their part.

Don't wait to call your subcontractors the evening before they are scheduled to arrive and inform them that your project is running five days behind schedule. Call them as soon as you see a possible delay developing. The more advance notice you can give, the better likelihood that your subs can work around the delay. This will reduce the chance of additional setbacks and a possible "domino effect" on your entire schedule.

GET OUT OF THE WORKER'S FACE BUT NEVER OUT OF HIS WAY

You've gotten some of your shopping out of the way, you have properly scheduled your subcontractors, and the work has finally begun on your project. It's full speed ahead, and everyone has their assignments. To know if the job is being done properly and according to your high expectations, you will need to establish good lines of communication with your workers.

The relationship between you and your subcontractors will be interesting, to say the least. In many respects, this relationship will be much like that of a good marriage. You will be seeing each other every day and will exist under the same roof together, albeit for a short while. There will be times when you are not completely happy with one another. In all probability, you will argue about many things. You will need to work at your relationship and develop a mutual trust for one another.

I have heard the argument that it's acceptable not to get along too well with your subcontractors. "If their personalities don't sit well with yours, it's no problem!" "After all, you are paying them for their skills as tradesmen and not to win any personality contests." "Contractors are a gruff, ornery bunch and they like to cuss and spit a lot and that's okay just as long as they do their job." Or so the arguments go.

You had better forget about all the stereotypes you've heard about contractors and welcome yourself into the 1990s. There are plenty of good workers out there who have a great deal of personality and social skills. It is up to you to find people who are compatible with you and capable of accepting your input and direction. This doesn't mean that you need to become best buddies with one another. It simply means that you will be working together for an extended period, and it is much more beneficial and productive to keep the lines of communication open. You don't want to have someone in there who doesn't care what you think as long as contractual responsibilities are met. By the same token, you have to be respectful of your workers' positions too.

An old joke among tradesmen says: "If you continually watch me while I work, I will charge you double. If you insist on helping me, your cost will be triple." This witticism is not without some wisdom. After all, no one wants their work scrutinized every minute of every day. How do you think you would feel if your boss were to put a surveillance camera on you and constantly watched while you worked? It would certainly make you feel uncomfortable, and your tradesmen are no different. Even though their work may be fascinating to you, allow them to get on with the job and don't impede progress with a constantly disruptive presence. It's all right to observe occasionally, but don't hover over them while they work.

The second part of the joke about helping them can be another problem. We talked earlier about it not being the tradesman's responsibility to teach you everything he knows. In your eagerness to help, remember to exercise some restraint so as not to be a nuisance rather than an asset. Tradesmen have the expertise and have developed their own sense of rhythm, and they don't need you to slow them down. Know what your role is and what you can comfortably do and are not capable of doing. There's a great line from a Clint Eastwood movie in which he says "a man has got to know his limitations." Just learn to be honest about your own.

There will be times, and you will develop a sense of just when that will be, when you have to interject and perhaps redirect a worker's efforts. On many occasions, decisions will have to be made that could not have been foreseen during the initial planning stages of your project. If you are not available to make those decisions, the tradesman or other workers may simply assume that they know what you would want. Such a decision may not be the one that you would have made, and it might be too late to do anything about it. Let your people know that you must be consulted before they make any decisions other than very minor ones.

Feel free to ask questions if something does not look right. Don't just yield to subs because they are the so-called "experts." You will begin to develop a gut feeling when the way something is being done does not look correct to you. Be careful not to be so wary of staying out of workers' way that you begin to miss things that should require your comments or questions. Use your common sense here.

DON'T BE AFRAID TO GET YOUR SHOES DIRTY

As we have explained and demonstrated to our workers many times, they worked "with" us and not "for" us. This is an important distinction. Your workers will have infinitely more respect for you if they know you are willing to get your shoes dirty.

Part of understanding your role as the manager of your project is to be aware of how you want your workers to perceive you. Will they think of you as a "little general" who parades around, barking out orders and commands and delegating responsibility and blame to others? Or, are they more likely to view you in the other extreme? Will your workers perceive you as being timid, weak, and just ripe to be taken advantage of? Will you be a leader and inspire or will you be a complainer and demoralize? It is really up to you.

Although it may sound a little corny, your workers will look to you for leadership. You may not be aware of it, but they will be looking nonetheless. Keep in mind that you control the purse strings and that makes you a very important player to the people on your team. You are "the boss," and you have a choice as to how you exercise that power.

One of the best examples that I have ever read about earned respect for leadership was written by John Leppelman in his book *Blood on the Risers: An Airborne Soldier's Thirty-five Months in Vietnam.* He writes:

> The rest of the afternoon was spent drinking beer and playing basketball with the platoon. We had our shirts off and were passing the ball around when up walked Colonel Sigholtz. I had already learned that most officers were nothing but trouble, and the best bet was to avoid them if possible. We got quiet, and Welch held the ball, stopping the game. The colonel walked up, looked us over, and said, "Is there room for one more in the game?"
>
> We quickly said there was. He stripped his shirt off and walked onto the court. He played basketball with us for about ten minutes, and he wasn't bad. I would never forget the colonel who could drop his birds and join the enlisted men. My respect for the man increased greatly after that incident.*

If you don't think that it's important to gain the respect of your workers by getting your shoes dirty, you are going to be in for a big surprise. You don't have to go in there and begin hanging ceiling joists or install the plumbing fixtures all by yourself just to prove that you are *with* your workers. I'm talking about gaining their respect by demonstrating a willingness to do whatever you can to help, without being in the way. You should, of course, be firm when necessary and not allow your workers to take advantage of you or your inexperience. Both these factors are integral components of your leadership responsibility.

There are many ways that you might motivate your workers into giving you their best work, such as being available to run out for more needed materials on short notice, showing a willingness to be an extra "hand" when necessary, passing up a sheet of plywood, or perhaps offering to walk out to their truck to fetch a tool. It also can't hurt to buy them a lunch or perhaps a six-pack or two for them to consume at home after the

---

* From *Blood on the Risers: An Airborne Soldier's Thirty-five Months in Vietnam*, copyright 1991 by John Leppelman, Ivy Books, published by Ballantine Books. Used with permission.

work week is finished and to compliment them at the end of each day for a job well done. Everyone responds favorably to sincere praise.

If you treat your workers with respect and loyalty you will get the best out of them because they will know that you are not the kind of person who complains about everything and begrudgingly writes out their checks. Showing workers your sincere respect almost always becomes a two-way street.

WHAT TO DO IF YOU ARE NOT SATISFIED WITH THE WAY SOMETHING HAS BEEN DONE

From time to time during the remodeling of your home you are going to come across things that have not been done to your satisfaction. The best way to guarantee that the job will ultimately be performed to your expectations is by holding back a portion of the final payment, as discussed in Chapter 4. By doing so, you will undoubtedly ensure better cooperation from your subcontractors.

Once you have the tradesmen's attention by withholding that final check, all you have to do if you are unhappy with any part of the job is to have the responsible parties make it right, no matter what or how long it takes to do so. You have been paying for them to do the job properly, and it is their obligation to see to it that it is.

If the toilet leaks one week after your plumber installed it, have him rip it out and find out why. Should you find that your drywall joint tape is visible after your painter has applied the primer coat, get the subcontractor back in and have him sand it down some more. Don't let your painter tell you that he can fix it but that it will have to be "extra." You certainly should never have to pay extra because another tradesman didn't do the job that he was paid to do.

What if the job has been done according to specifications and you still are not happy with it? Suppose that when you ultimately see how something will look, you just don't like it? It is perfectly okay to make changes once the project is underway. In some instances you may have to negotiate a revised price, but you definitely have the right to make those changes. If they do not substantially alter what has already been done or if you can foresee the changes far enough in advance, it may not even be necessary to incur additional costs. You and your subcontractor might agree that the change does not warrant any additional expenditures of time and money.

By being there to supervise your workers or, at the very least, carefully reviewing progress at each day's end you can exert much greater control over any plan alterations you may want to make as you go along. You certainly give yourself greater flexibility should you decide to change your mind about the way something was originally planned. It is far easier and less expensive to make changes early on rather than to wait until after that part of the project has been completed.

REVIEW

- Compare the material prices you obtain with those provided by your tradesman.

- Consider hiring moonlighting workers for greater savings.

- Prepare a complete and detailed materials list for each phase of the project before you shop.

- Take responsibility for having the materials delivered just before they will be needed.

- Act as a "general contractor" and expect the same treatment as such a professional.

- Buy from wholesale suppliers where practical.

- Always negotiate a builder's discount from all retail suppliers.

- Develop a detailed written schedule.

- Maintain some flexibility on your schedule and expect delays.

- Provide your subcontractors with as much advanced notice as possible when delays occur.

- Insist that your subcontractor supply you with his "A-Team" of best workers when needed.

- Develop good working relationships and keep lines of communication open.

- Recognize your own limitations and avoid slowing down the work progress.

- Insist that you be consulted before all but minor decisions are made.

- Think about how you want to be perceived as a leader.

- Gain the respect of your workers by not being afraid to get your shoes dirty.

- Treat your workers with respect and loyalty and expect the same in return.

- Be there to make changes, and the sooner the better.

Surviving the Remodeling Process

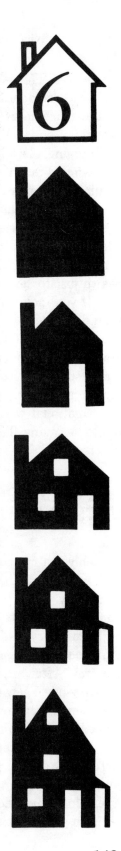

I started this book by talking about how difficult the entire remodeling process would be. If you are already underway, you will know what I was referring to. But in addition to all the headaches, no-shows, delays, excuses, cost overruns, oversights, and exhaustion, you can also look forward to experiencing pride, excitement, elation, and a great deal of personal satisfaction. Remodeling your home truly is all these things. You just have to believe that you will get through it and live to tell your story.

DON'T TAKE ON MORE THAN YOU ARE CAPABLE OF HANDLING

Most of us find ourselves in the habit of taking on more work than we should reasonably undertake in our lives. This is where some people tend to get into trouble when they decide to remodel their home. They anticipate that they will be able to devote much more time and energy to the project than they are truly capable of doing. You may find yourself saying: "Oh, I can do the painting [digging, electrical, plumbing, insulation, etc.] myself on my days off and when I'm on vacation." Most of these tasks take far longer and require much more energy than you might expect.

Your health also may prevent you from taking on certain aspects of the project yourself. It is probably a very good idea to talk with your doctor and to undergo a complete physical before taking on physically demanding work. You certainly would not want to be careless with your health just to save a few dollars on your remodeling.

If you included a subcontractor's bid in your original estimates, you should be able to cover yourself financially if you eventually discover that you really can't do it all. If you get into the project and decide that you are unable to undertake all you had originally intended to do yourself, hire a subcontractor to handle it for you. It is never too late to call in a pro. It may end up costing you more money, but in this case your health and emotional well-being are far more important than the money you would be saving. Take on only as much as you can comfortably handle.

ASK YOUR SPOUSE TO SQUINT UNTIL THE WORK IS FINISHED

Probably the most difficult part of the remodeling process for most couples is their ability to have faith that all the work will get done—eventually. When your house is "laid bare" in its primitive skeletal condition, you must have a great deal of imagination to "see" the end result. You begin to worry and to ask yourself ". . . how in the world are we ever going to get this back together?" It is normal and natural for people to feel this way. After all, your house wasn't like this when you bought it. You probably never saw all the wires, pipes, studs, floorboards, holes, and various other "inner workings" of your home. Now you do, and it can be a very unsettling experience.

You have to remember, too, that it takes time, a lot of time, to complete your project. I have already said that, depending on the extent of your plans, you can expect the whole process to take from six months to a year for completion. That's a long time to be unsettled! You will likely begin to get impatient. It's only natural, then, to begin to ask questions such as: "What are they going to do about that thing, there?" and "Do you think they forgot to attach that pipe?" or "They're not going to leave it like that, are they?"

While it is perfectly acceptable to ask each other these questions, it is best to take a "wait and see" attitude when you are dealing with the tradesmen. It is unreasonable for you to feel that you should understand exactly what's going to happen next at any given point in your project. To some extent, you just have to trust that your workers know what they are doing. There is really nothing to be gained by slowing down a professional with a lot of questions whose answers will become apparent as the job takes its course. I discussed the need for asking questions in the preceding chapter, but only in relation to making sure that the builder is following your plans and doing the work properly. Questions about each detail will, in almost all cases, be answered in due time through the results and will have no effect on the project's final outcome.

To keep the job progressing smoothly, just ask your spouse to squint until the work has been completed, and try to do the same yourself.

WEIGH ALL THE ADVICE BUT PADDLE YOUR OWN CANOE

A funny thing happens when you begin a remodeling project. Suddenly, everyone you have ever known along with everyone you then meet becomes an expert in giving remodeling advice. These well-meaning people just can't wait to tell you what they think you should do about this and just how you should change that. Everybody has an opinion and a ready willingness to express it. Believe it or not, this can be very good for both you and your project.

You have to understand that remodeling, to some degree, should be a group effort. No one person can come up with all the good ideas necessary to create something really special. It takes input from a lot of people and professionals to ensure a successful outcome to your remodeling project. I have said many times throughout this book that you do not and should not operate in a vacuum. You need people to give you input. Don't ever be afraid to ask your tradesmen to give you theirs.

Once during a remodeling project I was working on, a neighbor and I were talking and he said, "You know, you really should take pictures of everything while the interior walls are still exposed." A simple little suggestion, a harmless piece of advice, and it turned out to be one of the most important suggestions we have ever received during remodeling. I took my neighbor's advice and I cannot begin to tell you how many times it saved us from extra work.

The photos allowed us to find two electrical boxes that had been "buried" by the drywall. Without the snapshots, we would have otherwise been knocking holes in the drywall to find the boxes. To make matters worse, these missing boxes went undiscovered until the finish electrical phase of the project and long after the drywall contractor had left. Hunting for the boxes without our photos would have meant additional time and expense for patching. By studying the pictures, we had our answers and were able to "hit" those boxes without the need for additional patching.

Having a complete set of photographs can be very helpful in discovering plumbing problems as well. You only think you will remember the path every plumbing line took through your house. Once those walls are closed up, you won't have a clue. If your finish carpenter drives a nail through an ABS plastic soil stack while installing molding and you develop a bad smell throughout the house, you will be very happy to know *exactly* where those lines are located.

Take pictures of everything and from every angle: all ceilings, floors, walls, stairwells, closets, basements, roofs, and attics. The best time to take them will be after the rough plumbing, rough electrical work, and heating and air-conditioning plenum and return routing have been installed and before any of the walls have been insulated or sealed.

Of course, along with the good advice, you'll hear plenty of not-so-good advice. Before we began a major remodeling project as the "general contractors," we heard arguments such as: "Oh you really don't want to be your own general contractor, most professional general contractors have a 'lock' on all the good subcontractors. You simply won't be able to find any really good ones because they are only loyal to the 'generals' who keep them steadily employed. Even if the good subcontractors come to work for you, they will drop you flat if another job offered by the 'general' comes up."

While this argument is not without some merit, it is an extreme overgeneralization of this potential problem. Some subcontractors are very loyal to the general contractors who regularly employ them, but this doesn't mean that they won't work for someone who is serving as his own "general." It simply means that you have to be willing to "dig" a little deeper to find the right ones for you. If you are offering to employ someone, you can find excellent artisans who are loyal only to the person currently signing their paychecks. They generally don't care whether you are in the regular business of "general contracting" or are completing a one-time project. You will find this particularly true during these difficult economic times in the home building/remodeling industry.

It is your job to weigh each of the suggestions given to you and decide what will best suit your needs. You should expect that many well-meaning people will give you input with which you disagree. The important thing to remember here is that the decision on any matter relating to your project is in your hands. You will be the one responsible for deciding what is most appropriate for your particular situation. Remember to be clear in your objectives and not to allow anyone to convince you to accept other than what you want, since *you* will eventually live with the results. This can happen during a project when decisions have to be made quickly. Don't allow yourself to be rushed into making an unfortunate choice with long-term consequences.

WHEN THINGS ARE GOING ALL WRONG, JUST RUN AWAY

Part of the difficulty with supervising your own project is your direct emotional involvement with the undertaking. This is *your* home. You take great pride in seeing to it that everything turns out perfectly. It is solely your responsibility, you feel, to stay on top of every minute detail. If something goes wrong, it's easy to blame yourself. You are sure to have days where nothing goes according to plan. Tensions are heightened and tempers, including your own, may flare up. You may have hit that place where you find yourself asking: "What else could possibly go wrong today?"

There is a very simple solution to this problem. It is so simple, in fact, that you will wonder why you didn't think of it sooner. Just close the project down and send everybody home for the rest of that day. Think of it as a "cooling-off" period for everyone, and send them all away. By the way, "everyone" includes you, too. Force yourself to physically leave your home/project for the remainder of that day. Go do something that is completely removed from what you have been doing. See a movie or take your family to dinner or to the bowling alley and have a little diversionary fun. Do not allow yourself to think about the project until the following day. It will still be there tomorrow.

This maneuver may sound a little silly to you, but it is therapeutic and necessary to restore your sense of objectivity. When and if you ever feel that you, the project, or your workers are getting out of hand, it really is a viable solution. Professional diplomats and negotiators will often effect a cooling-off period to quell tempers and get things back on track. Surely you have heard of this happening during union negotiations. When representatives from both management and labor have reached an impasse and heated words have been exchanged, the president will occasionally be forced to call in a federal mediator whose responsibility is to break the impasse and force both sides to come to a reasonable agreement. This mediator will often call for an immediate cooling-off period and will send both sides away from the bargaining table for a certain length of time. This interval is intended to force all the parties involved to step back from the matter long enough to acquire a new perspective.

You and the people who work with you may require the same thing. Because you are so emotionally close to the project, sometimes you just need to step back from it long enough to obtain that new perspective. Don't be too concerned about falling behind on your schedule. If it becomes necessary for you to close down the job, it generally will not happen in the morning when people are still fresh. Chances are that the crisis will occur in the late afternoon when it is hot and everyone is tired and a bit stressed out. Your workers probably won't complain at the prospect of knocking off a little early anyway.

While things may never get so rough that it becomes necessary to close down your project, at least you can know that the option is available to you. Don't hesitate to consider it if the need should arise.

MAINTAIN YOUR BALANCE AND A SENSE OF HUMOR

A key factor in surviving your remodeling process is maintaining your balance and remembering to have a sense of humor. Remodeling can be richly rewarding, so you may as well enjoy the process. It is not about constantly getting upset, and feeling uptight and stressed all the time. Many things about the undertaking can be humorous.

You will surely make some mistakes so be willing to laugh at yourself. Don't beat yourself up over the silly oversights and errors you might make. Remodeling is a learning process, and you cannot expect to do everything perfectly on your first project. Even the professionals make mistakes, and they have been doing it a lot longer than you have.

Remember to maintain your sense of humor not only about yourself but also about those who will work with you. Keep a relaxed balance while achieving your objectives and by all means, have some fun!

REVIEW

- Don't take on more than you are capable of handling.

- Consult with your doctor before taking on any physically demanding work.

- Maintain your patience and ask your family to squint until the work is done.

- Remember that remodeling is a group effort so listen to the advice of others.

- Carefully weigh the advice of others and then make your own decisions.

- Always take detailed pictures of everything while the interior walls are visible.

- Be clear in your objectives.

- Don't let anyone talk you into something you really don't want.

- Close down your project for the remainder of the day and send everyone, including yourself, away if it seems as if things are getting out of hand.

- Learn to relax and enjoy the process and maintain your sense of humor.

Remodeling: The Aftermath

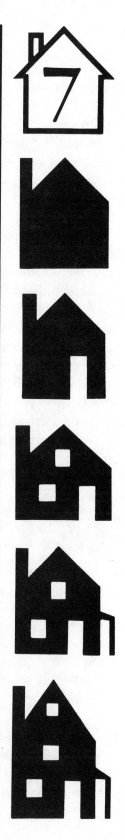

L ong after your remodeling project has ended and you prepare to sell your home, you will find that you must face some accounting issues that have arisen as a result of your efforts. While it is always a good idea for you to consult with a tax professional, here are some basics you should understand about the effects your home improvements will have on your taxes.

THE EFFECT OF IMPROVEMENTS ON YOUR HOME'S COST BASIS WHEN YOU SELL

In Chapter 3, I discussed the tax issues surrounding mortgage interest deductions. The tax issues I will talk about here are of an entirely different nature and should be considered when you begin the process of selling your home.

Nothing you will do by way of home improvements and their expenditures are tax deductible to you for the year in which they were paid except in the case of rental property. The federal government does not reward you with deductions for upgrading and improving your home. You cannot simply deduct all the costs of your project from your taxes in the year they were paid as you would a charitable contribution or a medical expense. It is perfectly acceptable, however, to increase the cost basis of your home by adding the "capital improvements" to what you paid for it. Take notice here that I said "improvements" and not "repairs." The Internal Revenue Service (IRS) makes a clear distinction here.

According to IRS Publication 530, repairs would include anything that "keeps your home in an ordinary efficient operating condition." The IRS goes on to explain that a repair ". . . does not add to the value of your home or prolong its life." "Repairs include repainting your home inside or outside, fixing your gutters or floors, fixing leaks or plastering, and replacing broken window panes." These items are not deductible to you unless your home is a rental property. There is one important exception, however. "Fixing-up" expenses can be subtracted from your capital gain if they occur within 90 days of the date when you actually sell your home. This means that if you repaint your home within 90 days of the time you sell, the cost is deductible along with your other closing costs.

The explanation continues by defining an improvement as anything that:

> . . . materially adds to the value of your home, considerably prolongs its useful life, or adapts it to new uses. . . . Improvements that you must add to the (cost) basis of your home include putting a recreation room in your unfinished basement, adding another bathroom or bedroom, putting up a fence, putting in new plumbing or (electrical, T.V., or monitor) wiring, installing a new roof, or paving your driveway. . . . Repairs that are done as part of *an extensive remodeling or restoration* of your home are considered improvements that must be added to the basis of your home.

Other items that would fall under improvements would be installations such as an in-ground swimming pool, underground sprinkler systems, outdoor lamps, built-ins such as cabinets and/or bookshelves, closet organizers, replacement windows, and new lighting fixtures. Planting new trees (not replacing old ones) and upgrading heating and air conditioning are also considered to be improvements.

The tests for the IRS as to whether or not something is considered to be an improvement is that you must design it to be permanent (lasting longer than one year); you can't take it with you when you sell (a portable wooden playhouse would probably not count as an improvement; however, a permanent toolshed would); and it must be comprehensive (replacing a single broken window pane would not count; however, replacing the entire window would). Of course you would always want to check with your accountant or the IRS if there is any question in your mind. You will need to know whether something is a capital improvement when it comes time to determine your home's cost basis.

Defining the Cost Basis

The cost basis is the actual amount that you paid for your home plus any capital improvements made during your ownership. Follow along with Figure 7–1, which is a reprint of IRS Form 2119, to understand just how this works.

As with the example in Chapter 3, let us assume that you purchased your home back in 1983 for $170,000. You have completed your recent remodeling project at a final cost of about $41,250. Since buying the home, you have made some other capital improvements over the years at a total cost of about $5,850. The total cost to you for your capital improvements was $47,100 ($41,250 + 5,850 = $47,100). We now add the cost of the improvements to the original purchase price to obtain a new cost basis of $217,100 ($170,000 + $47,100 = $217,100) and enter that amount on Line 7 of Form 2119.

In the spring of 1992, you sold your home for $277,000. We now enter this amount on Line 4. By selling the home, you incurred some closing costs for your legal fees and the commission paid to the real estate professional who helped accomplish the sale. Let us assume that these expenses amounted to $17,680. We enter that amount on Line 5. To determine the actual amount realized from the sale, we subtract $17,680 from $277,000 to arrive at $259,320. We then enter this amount on Line 6.

To determine the gain on the sale of the home we subtract our new cost basis of $217,100 from the amount realized of $259,320 to arrive at $42,220. We then enter the gain on Line 8a.

Figure 7–1

IRS Form 2119—Defining Cost Basis

Form **2119**

Department of the Treasury
Internal Revenue Service

Sale of Your Home

▶ Attach to Form 1040 for year of sale.

▶ See separate instructions. ▶ Please print or type.

OMB No. 1545-0072

1991

Attachment
Sequence No. **20**

Your first name and initial. (If joint return, also give spouse's name and initial.)	Last name	Your social security number

Fill in Your Address Only if You Are Filing This Form by Itself and Not With Your Tax Return	Present address (no., street, and apt. no., rural route, or P.O. box no. if mail is not delivered to street address)	Spouse's social security number
	City, town or post office, state, and ZIP code	

Caution: *If the home sold was financed (in whole or part) from a mortgage credit certificate or the proceeds of a tax-exempt qualified mortgage bond, you may owe additional tax. Get Form 8828, Recapture of Federal Mortgage Subsidy, for details.*

Part I General Information

1a Date your former main home was sold (month, day, year) · · · · · · · · · ▶ | 1a | 4 / 20 / 92

b Face amount of any mortgage, note (e.g., second trust), or other financial instrument on which you will get periodic payments of principal or interest from this sale (see instructions) · · · | 1b |

2 Have you bought or built a new main home? · · · · · · · · · · · · · · · · ☑ Yes ☐ No

3 Is or was any part of either main home rented out or used for business? (If "Yes," see instructions.) · · ☐ Yes ☑ No

Part II Gain on Sale (Do not include amounts you deduct as moving expenses.)

4 Selling price of home. (Do not include personal property items that you sold with your home.) | 4 | 277,000 —

5 Expense of sale. (Include sales commissions, advertising, legal, etc.) · · · · · · · | 5 | 17,680 —

6 Amount realized. Subtract line 5 from line 4 · · · · · · · · · · · · · | 6 | 259,320 —

7 Basis of home sold (see instructions) · · · · · · · · · · · · · · · | 7 | 217,100 —

8a Gain on sale. Subtract line 7 from line 6 · · · · · · · · · · · · · · | 8a | 42,220 —

- If line 8a is zero or less, stop here and attach this form to your return.
- If line 2 is "Yes," you **must** go to Part III or Part IV, whichever applies. Otherwise, go to line 8b.

b If you haven't replaced your home, do you plan to do so within the replacement period (see instructions)? ☐ Yes ☐ No

- If "Yes," stop here, attach this form to your return, and see **Additional Filing Requirements** in the instructions.
- If "No," you **must** go to Part III or Part IV, whichever applies.

Part III One-Time Exclusion of Gain for People Age 55 or Older (If you are not taking the exclusion, go to Part IV now.)

9a Who was age 55 or older on date of sale? · · · · · · · · · · · · ☐ You ☐ Your spouse ☐ Both of you

b Did the person who was age 55 or older own and use the property as his or her main home for a total of at least 3 years (except for short absences) during the 5-year period before the sale? (If "No," go to Part IV now.) ☐ Yes ☐ No

c If line 9b is "Yes," do you elect to take the one-time exclusion? (If "No," go to Part IV now.) ☐ Yes ☐ No

d At time of sale, who owned the home? · · · · · · · · · · · · ☐ You ☐ Your spouse ☐ Both of you

e Social security number of spouse at time of sale if you had a different spouse from the one above at time of sale. (If you were not married at time of sale, enter "None.") · · · · · ▶ | 9e |

f **Exclusion.** Enter the **smaller** of line 8a or $125,000 ($62,500, if married filing separate return) · | 9f |

Part IV Adjusted Sales Price, Taxable Gain, and Adjusted Basis of New Home

10 Subtract line 9f from line 8a · · · · · · · · · · · · · · · · · · | 10 | 42,220 —

- If line 10 is zero, stop here and attach this form to your return.
- If line 2 is "Yes," go to line 11 now.
- If you are reporting this sale on the installment method, stop here and see the line 1b instructions.
- All others, stop here and enter the amount from line 10 on Schedule D, line 2 or line 9.

11 Fixing-up expenses (see instructions for time limits) · · · · · · · · · · | 11 | 960 —

12 **Adjusted sales price.** Subtract line 11 from line 6 · · · · · · · · · · · | 12 | 258,360 —

13a Date you moved into new home (month, day, year) ▶ 4 / 20 / 92 **b** Cost of new home | 13b | 260,000 —

14a Add line 9f and line 13b · · · · · · · · · · · · · · · · · · · | 14a | 260,000 —

b Subtract line 14a from line 12. If the result is zero or less, enter -0- · · · · · · | 14b | -0-

c **Taxable gain.** Enter the **smaller** of line 10 or line 14b · · · · · · · · · | 14c | -0-

- If line 14c is zero, go to line 15 and attach this form to your return.
- If you are reporting this sale on the installment method, see the line 1b instructions and go to line 15.
- All others, enter the amount from line 14c on Schedule D, line 2 or line 9, and go to line 15.

15 Postponed gain. Subtract line 14c from line 10 · · · · · · · · · · · | 15 | 42,220 —

16 **Adjusted basis of new home.** Subtract line 15 from line 13b · · · · · · · · | 16 | 217,780 —

Sign Here Only If You Are Filing This Form by Itself and Not With Your Tax Return	Under penalties of perjury, I declare that I have examined this form, including attachments, and to the best of my knowledge and belief, it is true, correct, and complete.
	Your signature _____ Date _____ Spouse's signature _____ Date _____
	(If a joint return, both must sign.)

For Paperwork Reduction Act Notice, see separate instructions.   Cat. No. 11710J   Form **2119** (1991)

✭ U.S. GOVERNMENT PRINTING OFFICE: 1991- 285-288

For this exercise, let us assume that neither you nor your spouse are over 55 years of age and cannot exercise the one-time tax exclusion of $125,000. We will talk more about this option later in the chapter. For now, we will not check boxes on Lines 9a, b, c, and d.

In preparation for the sale of your home and within the 90-day period we spoke of before, you had your home repainted and some other minor cosmetic repairs made at a cost of $960. These "fixing-up" expenses have been entered on Line 11. We then subtract these expenses from the amount realized of $259,320 to arrive at an adjusted sale price of $258,360. This number is then entered on Line 12.

On April 20, 1992, you purchase a new home at a cost of $260,000. This information is entered onto Lines 13a and 13b. We then need to establish the taxable gain by first subtracting the cost of the new home from the adjusted sales price of the old. Since the number we arrive at is a negative number, we enter zero on Line 14b. Then, since we can all agree that zero is less than $42,220, we enter zero on Line 14c. We then enter $42,220 on Line 15.

We are now, in effect, postponing the gain on the sale of the old home because we have bought a new home for an amount greater than or equal to the adjusted sale price of the old. Under the rules provided by the IRS, this is perfectly acceptable. As long as you purchase or complete the building of your new principal residence within two years of the sale of your old home and for equal or greater value, you will have no problems with the IRS wanting any money now. However, there are provisions in the tax code to prevent you from postponing the gain when you sell the new home for a quick profit. As a general rule, you should plan on staying in the new home for at least two years before selling it if you plan to defer the gain. An exception to this is made for those people who are relocated due to a legitimate job transfer.

Many people have effectively postponed their capital gains on the sale of their principal residences to the point that they never pay any taxes on the gains during their lifetime. This doesn't mean that the tax won't eventually have to be paid, it just means that it can be postponed until the deaths of both spouses.

Nowhere does the IRS tell you that you must apply the cash proceeds from the sale of your old home toward the purchase of a new one, though. It is perfectly acceptable for you to borrow as much of the money needed for the purchase as you are able to. Remember that home mortgage interest is deductible if you meet certain criteria (see the section "The Tax Advantages of the Home Mortgage Interest Deduction," in Chapter 3). You can always use your cash proceeds for any purpose you wish, including the remodeling of your *new* home (see the section "Become Your Own Banker," in Chapter 3).

Purchasing the New Home for Less than the Adjusted Sales Price of the Old One

Our first example assumes that you bought a new home with a value greater than or equal to the adjusted sales price of your old home. Let us examine Figure 7-2 to see what would happen if you were to purchase a home of lesser value. For this example, let's assume that the new home you purchased cost $175,000 and that all other numbers were identical to those used in Figure 7-1 (Lines 1 through 12). What effect would this new scenario have on your capital gain taxes and your ability to postpone them?

In this case, you would be unable to postpone the gain and the taxes would be due for the year in which you sold your old home. We enter the purchase price for the new home on Line 13b of Form 2119 (Figure 7-2). Since once again we assume that we do not have the option of using the one-time $125,000 exclusion, we also have entered $175,000 on Line 14a. By subtracting the cost of the new home from the adjusted sales price of the old, we now have a difference of $83,360. We therefore enter this amount on Line 14b.

Since the $42,220 is the smaller of the two numbers in Lines 10 and 14b, we enter this amount on Line 14c. Now we know that $42,220 (Line 10) minus $42,220 (Line 14c) equals zero, so we determine that none of $42,220 can be postponed and enter zero on Line 15. Therefore, the adjusted basis for the new home is equal to its purchase price (Line 16). You will now owe taxes on the $42,220 gain from the sale of your old home.

Applying the One-Time $125,000 Exclusion

Let us now make the assumption that either you or your spouse has reached the age of 55 or older by the time that you sell your old home. Provided that you have used this home as your principal residence for at least three of the previous five years prior to the sale and that neither you nor your spouse has used the exclusion before, you may exclude all the gain up to a maximum of $125,000. You should be aware that at the time of this writing, there is pending legislation on Capitol Hill which would extend the current exclusion ceiling of $125,000 to

Figure 7–2

IRS Form 2119—Reporting Capital Gain

Form **2119**	**Sale of Your Home**	OMB No. 1545-0072
Department of the Treasury Internal Revenue Service	▶ **Attach to Form 1040 for year of sale.** ▶ **See separate instructions.** ▶ **Please print or type.**	**1991** Attachment Sequence No. **20**

Your first name and initial. (If joint return, also give spouse's name and initial.)	Last name	Your social security number
Fill in Your Address Only If You Are Filing This Form by Itself and Not With Your Tax Return	Present address (no., street, and apt. no., rural route, or P.O. box no. if mail is not delivered to street address)	Spouse's social security number
	City, town or post office, state, and ZIP code	

Caution: *If the home sold was financed (in whole or part) from a mortgage credit certificate or the proceeds of a tax-exempt qualified mortgage bond, you may owe additional tax. Get Form 8828, Recapture of Federal Mortgage Subsidy, for details.*

Part I   General Information

1a	Date your former main home was sold (month, day, year) . . . . ▶	1a	4 / 20 / 92
b	Face amount of any mortgage, note (e.g., second trust), or other financial instrument on which you will get periodic payments of principal or interest from this sale (see instructions) . . .	1b	
2	Have you bought or built a new main home?		☑ Yes ☐ No
3	Is or was any part of either main home rented out or used for business? (If "Yes," see instructions). .		☐ Yes ☑ No

Part II   Gain on Sale (Do not include amounts you deduct as moving expenses.)

4	Selling price of home. (Do not include personal property items that you sold with your home.)	4	277,000 —
5	Expense of sale. (Include sales commissions, advertising, legal, etc.)	5	17,680 —
6	Amount realized. Subtract line 5 from line 4	6	259,320 —
7	Basis of home sold (see instructions)	7	217,100 —
8a	Gain on sale. Subtract line 7 from line 6	8a	42,220 —

- If line 8a is zero or less, stop here and attach this form to your return.
- If line 2 is "Yes," you **must** go to Part III or Part IV, whichever applies. Otherwise, go to line 8b.

b	If you haven't replaced your home, do you plan to do so within the replacement period (see instructions)?		☐ Yes ☐ No

- If "Yes," stop here, attach this form to your return, and see **Additional Filing Requirements** in the instructions.
- If "No," you **must** go to Part III or Part IV, whichever applies.

Part III   One-Time Exclusion of Gain for People Age 55 or Older (If you are not taking the exclusion, go to Part IV now.)

9a	Who was age 55 or older on date of sale?.	☐ You ☐ Your spouse	☐ Both of you
b	Did the person who was age 55 or older own and use the property as his or her main home for a total of at least 3 years (except for short absences) of the 5-year period before the sale? (If "No," go to Part IV now.)		☐ Yes ☐ No
c	**If line 9b is "Yes," do you elect to take the one-time exclusion?** (If "No," go to Part IV now.) . . .		☐ Yes ☐ No
d	At time of sale, who owned the home?.	☐ You ☐ Your spouse	☐ Both of you
e	Social security number of spouse at time of sale if you had a different spouse from the one above at time of sale. (If you were not married at time of sale, enter "None.") . . .	9e	
f	**Exclusion.** Enter the **smaller** of line 8a or $125,000 ($62,500, if married filing separate return)	9f	

Part IV   Adjusted Sales Price, Taxable Gain, and Adjusted Basis of New Home

10	Subtract line 9f from line 8a	10	42,220 —

- If line 10 is zero, stop here and attach this form to your return.
- If line 2 is "Yes," go to line 11 now.
- If you are reporting this sale on the installment method, stop here and see the line 1b instructions.
- All others, stop here and **enter the amount from line 10 on Schedule D, line 2 or line 9.**

11	Fixing-up expenses (see instructions for time limits)	11	960 —
12	**Adjusted sales price.** Subtract line 11 from line 6	12	258,360 —
13a	Date you moved into new home (month, day, year) ▶	4 / 20 / 92	**b** Cost of new home	13b	175,000 —
14a	Add line 9f and line 13b	14a	175,000 —
b	Subtract line 14a from line 12. If the result is zero or less, enter -0-	14b	83,360 —
c	**Taxable gain.** Enter the **smaller** of line 10 or line 14b	14c	42,220 —

- If line 14c is zero, go to line 15 and attach this form to your return.
- If you are reporting this sale on the installment method, see the line 1b instructions and go to line 15.
- All others, enter the amount from line 14c on **Schedule D, line 2 or line 9,** and go to line 15.

15	Postponed gain. Subtract line 14c from line 10	15	-0-
16	**Adjusted basis of new home.** Subtract line 15 from line 13b	16	175,000 —

Sign Here Only If You Are Filing This Form by Itself and Not With Your Tax Return ▶	Under penalties of perjury, I declare that I have examined this form, including attachments, and to the best of my knowledge and belief, it is true, correct, and complete.
	Your signature _____ Date _____ Spouse's signature _____ Date _____ (If a joint return, both must sign.)

For Paperwork Reduction Act Notice, see separate instructions.   Cat. No. 11710J   Form **2119** (1991)

★ U.S. GOVERNMENT PRINTING OFFICE: 1991- 288-288

allow for inflation. Under this proposed plan, the current figure would be indexed to rise over the years to keep pace with the consumer price index. Check with your accountant or the IRS for the most current information on this and other federal tax code regulations.

Keep in mind here that this exclusion of the gain is available for your use for only one time in the lifetime of either you or your spouse, providing that one of you is 55 or older on the date of the sale. You cannot simply "save" part of the exclusion for use at another time. In other words, if in our previous example your gain was $42,220, one of you was in fact 55 or older, and you chose to exercise your exclusion on this event, your particular exclusion would be $42,220 and $82,780 in available exclusion would be lost forever.

You are not required to exercise your exclusion just because you qualify under the terms already discussed. It is acceptable and may be preferable for you to choose to retain your exclusion for a later primary home sale. Be cautious and consult with an accountant for expert advice before you exercise your right to the exclusion. It would also be very helpful for you to obtain and read IRS *Publication 523: Tax Information on Selling Your Home.* This and other IRS publications that we have discussed in this book are free and available directly from any IRS Forms Distribution Center or by calling the IRS toll free at 1-800-TAX-FORM (829-3676). It can sometimes take up to 10 days or more to have them mail you copies of these publications, so you may want to check with your local public library or your accountant to see if they have copies available for your review.

To examine an exercise that uses the exclusion effectively, follow along with Figure 7–3. For this example, our assumptions are that the selling price, expenses of the sale, fixing-up expenses, amount realized on the sale of the old home, and the price paid for the new home are identical to our first example. Only now, we are going to assume that instead of buying your old home in 1983 for $170,000, you bought it in 1975 for $88,000 and then proceeded over the years to add the improvements of $47,100. We now have a total of $135,100 for the basis of the home we are selling. List this amount on Line 7. Subtracting $135,100 from the realized amount on the sale of $259,320 leaves a gain of $124,220, which we enter on Line 8a.

Since both you and your spouse are 55 years old and intend to exercise your one-time exclusion, you check the "Both of you" box on Line 9a, yes on Lines 9b and c, and "Both of you" on Line 9d. Because your gain is slightly less than the $125,000, you enter $124,220 on Line 9f. Remember here, your exclusion is $125,000 or *less*. You have to use the lesser of the two numbers.

Figure 7–3

IRS Form 2119—Applying the One-Time Exclusion

Form **2119**	**Sale of Your Home**	OMB No. 1545-0072
Department of the Treasury Internal Revenue Service	▶ Attach to Form 1040 for year of sale. ▶ See separate instructions. ▶ Please print or type.	**19 91** Attachment Sequence No. **20**

Your first name and initial. (If joint return, also give spouse's name and initial.)   Last name | Your social security number

Fill in Your Address Only If You Are Filing This Form by Itself and Not With Your Tax Return	Present address (no., street, and apt. no., rural route, or P.O. box no. if mail is not delivered to street address)	Spouse's social security number
	City, town or post office, state, and ZIP code	

Caution: *If the home sold was financed (in whole or part) from a mortgage credit certificate or the proceeds of a tax-exempt qualified mortgage bond, you may owe additional tax. Get **Form 8828**, Recapture of Federal Mortgage Subsidy, for details.*

Part I General Information

1a	Date your former main home was sold (month, day, year) . . . . ▶	**1a**	4 / 20 / 92
b	Face amount of any mortgage, note (e.g., second trust), or other financial instrument on which you will get periodic payments of principal or interest from this sale (see instructions) . . .	**1b**	
2	Have you bought or built a new main home?		☑ Yes ☐ No
3	Is or was any part of either main home rented out or used for business? (If "Yes," see instructions.) . .		☐ Yes ☑ No

Part II Gain on Sale (Do not include amounts you deduct as moving expenses.)

4	Selling price of home. (Do not include personal property items that you sold with your home.)	**4**	277,000 —
5	Expense of sale. (Include sales commissions, advertising, legal, etc.)	**5**	17,680 —
6	Amount realized. Subtract line 5 from line 4	**6**	259,320 —
7	Basis of home sold (see instructions)	**7**	135,100 —
8a	**Gain on sale.** Subtract line 7 from line 6	**8a**	124,220 —

• If line 8a is zero or less, stop here and attach this form to your return.
• If line 2 is "Yes," you **must** go to Part III or Part IV, whichever applies. Otherwise, go to line 8b.

b If you haven't replaced your home, do you plan to do so within the replacement period (see instructions)?   ☐ Yes ☐ No
• If "Yes," stop here, attach this form to your return, and see **Additional Filing Requirements** in the instructions.
• If "No," you **must** go to Part III or Part IV, whichever applies.

Part III One-Time Exclusion of Gain for People Age 55 or Older (If you are not taking the exclusion, go to Part IV now.)

9a	Who was age 55 or older on date of sale?	☐ You ☐ Your spouse	☑ Both of you
b	Did the person who was age 55 or older own and use the property as his or her main home for a total of at least 3 years (except for short absences) of the 5-year period before the sale? (If "No," go to Part IV now.)		☑ Yes ☐ No
c	**If line 9b is "Yes,"** do you elect to take the one-time exclusion? (If "No," go to Part IV now.) . . .		☑ Yes ☐ No
d	At time of sale, who owned the home?	☐ You ☐ Your spouse	☑ Both of you
e	Social security number of spouse at time of sale if you had a different spouse from the one above at time of sale. (If you were not married at time of sale, enter "None.") . . . . . ▶	**9e**	
f	**Exclusion.** Enter the **smaller** of line 8a or $125,000 ($62,500, if married filing separate return)	**9f**	124,220 —

Part IV Adjusted Sales Price, Taxable Gain, and Adjusted Basis of New Home

10	Subtract line 9f from line 8a	**10**	–0–

• If line 10 is zero, stop here and attach this form to your return.
• If line 2 is "Yes," go to line 11 now.
• If you are reporting this sale on the installment method, stop here and see the line 1b instructions.
• All others, stop here and **enter the amount from line 10 on Schedule D, line 2 or line 9.**

11	Fixing-up expenses (see instructions for time limits)	**11**	960 —
12	**Adjusted sales price.** Subtract line 11 from line 6	**12**	258,360 —
13a	Date you moved into new home (month, day, year) ▶ 4 / 20 / 92 **b** Cost of new home	**13b**	260,000 —
14a	Add line 9f and line 13b	**14a**	384,220 —
b	Subtract line 14a from line 12. If the result is zero or less, enter -0-	**14b**	–0–
c	**Taxable gain.** Enter the **smaller** of line 10 or line 14b	**14c**	–0–

• If line 14c is zero, go to line 15 and attach this form to your return.
• If you are reporting this sale on the installment method, see the line 1b instructions and go to line 15.
• All others, **enter the amount from line 14c on Schedule D, line 2 or line 9,** and go to line 15.

15	Postponed gain. Subtract line 14c from line 10	**15**	–0–
16	**Adjusted basis of new home.** Subtract line 15 from line 13b	**16**	260,000 —

Sign Here Only If You Are Filing This Form by Itself and Not With Your Tax Return	Under penalties of perjury, I declare that I have examined this form, including attachments, and to the best of my knowledge and belief, it is true, correct, and complete.
	Your signature Date Spouse's signature Date
	▶ ▶
	(If a joint return, both must sign.)

For Paperwork Reduction Act Notice, see separate instructions.   Cat. No. 11710J   Form **2119** (1991)

★U.S. GOVERNMENT PRINTING OFFICE: 1991- 285-288

We now complete the exercise by subtracting the fixing-up expenses from the amount realized from the sale of the old house to arrive at $258,360 (259,320 − 960 = $258,360). This number is then listed on Line 12 followed by the purchase price of the new home, $260,000, on Line 13b.

Because we have exercised our one-time exclusion, our taxable gain is zero, no taxes are owed, and no gain has been postponed in this example. Therefore, on the new home the adjusted basis is the same as the cost, $260,000.

Reasonable Conclusions

What conclusions can be drawn from our examples here and how do they relate to the remodeling of your home? In Chapter 3, I mentioned the importance of saving receipts acquired during your remodeling project. You need these receipts to determine the new basis of your home. You could probably take an educated guess by adding up the personal checks you wrote during the project and come pretty close, but what if you remodeled 5 or 10 years ago? Odds are that you won't remember what every check was written for way back then, and the IRS is not all that interested in guesses. If you ever face an audit, you had better be able to prove what you spent on improvements. *Save all your home improvement receipts!*

In addition to saving receipts, I strongly recommend that you keep a running tally of these expenditures on worksheets such as the ones illustrated in Figures 7–4 and 7–5. The costs of labor and materials are recorded on separate worksheets, to be consistent with what we have tried to do all along. Even though you will have saved all the receipts together in one place, it's a good idea to write out what each was for while it is still fresh in your mind. Don't wait until four or five years after you have remodeled to try and remember how much money you spent and for which projects. It will be much easier for you just to pick up the tally sheets for the quick answers you will need.

Be prepared to hang onto your home improvement receipt records for quite a long while. Exactly how long the IRS expects you to do this is unclear. However, you can expect that they might be needed long after you sell the home and end up deferring your gain. While the statute of limitations is generally considered to be three years from the date of filing your Form 2119 (filed along with your regular Form 1040 for the year in which

Figure 7–4

Cost Worksheet (Labor and Services)

HOME IMPROVEMENT COSTS - LABOR & SERVICES

Date	Code	Description	Check # or "Cash"	Amount	Totals

Code Key:

P = Plumbing	LE = Legal	F = Floor Work	SW = Stair Work
E = Electrical	A = Architectural	L = Landscaping	S = Septic Work
GL = General Labor	RC = Rough Carpentry	C = Concrete Work	M = Miscellaneous
R = Roofing	FC = Finish Carpentry	PA = Painting	
MA = Masonry	EW = Ext. Wall Siding	WP = Wallpapering	
DP = Drywall/Plaster	DR = Debris Removal	PD = Professional Decorator	
I = Insurance	T = Tile Work	MW = Metal Work	

Figure 7–5

Worksheet (Materials)

HOME IMPROVEMENT COSTS - MATERIALS

Date	Code	Description	Check # or "Cash"	Amount	Totals

Code Key:

PF=Plumbing & Fixtures	D=Doors	LM=Landscaping Material
EF=Electrical & Fixtures	MM=Masonry Material	PM=Painting Material
L=Lumber	ID=Insulation & Deadening	WM=Wallpaper Material
H=Hardware	DP=Drywall/Plaster	MI=Mirrors
CM=Concrete Material	CA=Cabinets	SD=Shower Doors
RM=Roofing Material	SM=Stair Material	OD=Other Decorating Material
W=Windows	TM=Tile Material	M=Miscellaneous

you sold your house), it couldn't hurt to hold onto them for longer than that. According to IRS *Publication 530:* "You must usually keep records to support deductions for at least 3 years from the date the return was filed, or 2 years from the time you paid the tax, whichever is later, or for as long as they are important for tax purposes." Since the last phrase makes a time period hard to pin down, it is best to be cautious and preserve your records forever.

One side note for you to keep in mind here is that *you cannot include the cost of your time when calculating home improvement costs for IRS reporting.* For example, assume that you are an attorney and, in the course of your practice, you customarily bill out your time at $125 per hour. You than calculate that you have spent nearly 200 billable hours away from your professional practice because of the work you were doing on your home remodeling project. You cannot just throw in a receipt for your time of $25,000 and expect to add it to your home improvement costs. The IRS will not allow it. They simply do not place a value on the time you spent working on the remodeling of your own home. We know, however, just how valuable your time can really be. The rewards for your time spent will come from the money you saved by doing it yourself.

Also remember the rule that prevents you from postponing the gains made from quick profit. You cannot simply sell your old home, purchase and immediately remodel a new one, and then turn around and sell it within two years for a quick profit and still expect to take advantage of postponing the gain. The IRS will disallow it, so be sure to consider this factor when timing your sale. It will become particularly important if you should decide to remodel again for fun and profit. *Don't sell your new home for at least two years if you wish to take advantage of postponing the taxable gain.*

What about the repairs that you want to be considered as "fixing-up costs"? Remember that you cannot include the cost of "repairs" in adding up your home's cost basis. Only improvements are considered. Fixing-up costs, however, can be considered when determining your home's adjusted sales price. Therefore, *postpone needed repairs to within 90 days of the sale of your home.*

Something else to consider is your awareness of the time deadlines involved with the taxable gain postponement options. You already know that you have up to 24 months either to buy or build and occupy a new principal residence in order to take advantage of the rollover on your taxable gain. Remember, there are no extensions to this time limit. If you buy a new home even one day beyond 24 months, you will have to pay taxes on the entire taxable gain for the year in which you sold your old home.

The problem gets even more complicated if you decide to build or remodel the new home that you buy. If you face delays in the completion and occupancy of your new home, even if they are beyond your control, you are out of luck in your pleadings with the IRS. Here again, you must have spent the money totaling an amount greater than or equal to the adjusted sales price of the old home, and you must have occupied that new home within 24 months of the sale of the old one to postpone the taxable gain. No exceptions! Just be sure that you *remember the 24-month rule and plan accordingly.*

Take advantage of the one-time $125,000 exclusion if you qualify and if your analysis proves that it is the right time to exercise this option. With the example we went over in Figure 7–3, you can see that this would be an appropriate time. You can effectively avoid paying any taxes on a maximum of $125,000 of your gain if you qualify under the rules.

Unless you have the advantage of avoiding taxable gains through use of the exclusion, *always buy or build a new home for an amount greater than or equal to the adjusted sales price of the one you sold.* As we have already discussed, this allows you to postpone the entire taxable gain. This, of course, assumes that your current financial position and employment status permit you to do so. Also, *consider the possibility of borrowing the maximum affordable amount against the new home and save your cash proceeds from the sale of the old one for other investments.*

Remember, the IRS does not stipulate that you must apply the sale proceeds to the purchase of a new home. That money might best be invested elsewhere for a greater return.

Once again, *in all matters relating to financial strategies or tax matters involving the sale of your home, you should always check with your accountant, tax advisor, or, if necessary, directly with the IRS to determine the most practical course for you to take.*

IT'S OVER AT LAST (I THOUGHT THIS DAY WOULD NEVER COME)

At last the sounds of hammering, sawing, and banging are finally silenced. No more continuous and extraordinary drain on your checkbook.

No more bothersome schedules to meet. No more annoying delays. No more strangers intruding on your privacy. No more dust and dirt. It's over at last! Peace and quiet have returned, or at least things are back to normal. Your home belongs, once again, to just you and your family.

What do you have when it's all over? You have the pride in knowing that you have done your best. You've earned your place among those who have built something that will stand long after they are gone. You've earned bragging rights with all your friends and can proudly show them what you as a family have accomplished. Let them see for themselves what a first-class home remodeling looks like. When they have gone, enjoy it for yourselves. You deserve it!

HOW WELL DID YOU DO?

When you have finished your project, it is fun to figure out how much money you saved by doing some of the work yourself, acting as your own general contractor, and buying your own materials. Back in Chapter 2, you will recall that we assembled a Contractor's Estimate Sheet to determine how much the whole project would cost. In building those estimates, we used numbers provided by the various subcontractors to be sure that there would be a sufficient financial "cushion." Now it is time to find out how well you did by comparing your original projected estimates with your actual final costs.

There are really two reasons for undergoing an exercise such as the one illustrated in Figure 7–6. The first is so that you can find out in which areas you went over budget and try to figure out why. This will help you in budgeting for your next remodeling, should you decide to undertake another project some day. And second, you will want to determine a value for the amount of time you spent on the work. Remember, you cannot add the value of your time to the cost basis of your home for tax purposes, but you can determine just how much money you saved for your own information. After all, we already know that the money you save is money you have earned.

Something that cannot be measured on any sheet of paper is the personal satisfaction gained by accomplishing what you have set out to do. You and your family have planned and executed your home remodeling project and can now sit back and enjoy the fruits of your labor. You have earned that much-needed rest.

Figure 7–6

Worksheet for Comparing Estimates with Final Costs

YOUR HOME REMODELING PROJECT
PROJECTED vs. ACTUAL COSTS

ITEM DESCRIPTION	PROJECTED COSTS	ACTUAL COSTS	SAVINGS/ <LOSS>
PLANS, SPECIFICATIONS & ENGINEERING			
BUILDING PERMITS			
INSURANCE			
TEMPORARY STORAGE			
TEMPORARY HOUSING			
DEMOLITION			
REMOVING DEBRIS			
EXCAVATION			
CONCRETE FOUNDATION			
CONCRETE FINISH			
ROUGH CARPENTRY			
FINISH CARPENTRY			
ROUGH LUMBER			
FINISH LUMBER			
ROUGH HARDWARE			
MASONRY			
ROUGH PLUMBING (LABOR & MATERIALS)			
FINISH PLUMBING (LABOR)			
PLUMBING FIXTURES & MATERIAL			
SEWER/CESSPOOL			
HEATING & AIR CONDITIONING			
ROUGH ELECTRICAL (LABOR)			
FINISH ELECTRICAL (LABOR)			
ELECTRICAL FIXTURES & ALL MATERIALS			
SHEET METAL (LABOR & MATERIALS)			
ROOF (LABOR)			
ROOF (MATERIALS)			
WINDOWS			
DOORS			
INSULATION (LABOR & MATERIALS)			
EXTERIOR SIDING (LABOR & MATERIALS)			
INTERIOR DRYWALL/PLASTER (LABOR)			
INTERIOR DRYWALL/PLASTER (MATERIALS)			
CABINETS (LABOR & MATERIALS)			
STAIRS (LABOR & MATERIALS)			
TILE (LABOR)			
TILE (MATERIALS)			
FLOORING (LABOR & MATERIALS)			
SHOWER DOORS & MIRRORS			
CLEANUP (LABOR)			
LANDSCAPING (LABOR & MATERIALS)			
PAINTING (LABOR & MATERIALS)			
WALLPAPERING (LABOR & MATERIALS)			
DECORATING (MATERIALS)			
PROFESSIONAL DECORATOR			
MISCELLANEOUS			
TOTALS			

DOING IT AGAIN FOR FUN AND PROFIT

You may know of people who remodel their own homes primarily for profit. It is not at all unusual for people to buy a home, live there for a couple of years while they make the improvements, and then move on to the next home and remodeling project. This was okay when you could count on home appreciation rates of 10% or more a year, but things have changed.

As this book is being written, we find ourselves immersed in an economic recession. The resale housing market that flourished only a short time ago in places such as New York, California, Florida, Connecticut, and many other parts of the country has all but come to a grinding halt. In New England, for example, the depressed economic picture has almost devastated the real estate market. This, in turn, has caused the failure of a number of regional banks because they held many real estate assets that were forced into foreclosure. Some of the homeowners themselves, who once counted on appreciation and the strong equity position in their homes to sustain them through tough economic times, have found themselves having to "walk" from their homes, often at a substantial loss, because of their own economic hardships.

What do all these factors mean? There are many people who use the argument that it is time to "live" in our homes rather than to expect them to provide us with great wealth. These same people would argue that we will never again see double-digit real estate appreciation in *any* areas of the country. In fact, they would argue that we as home owners will be lucky to see any appreciation at all and should expect a decline in real estate values. Some people think that homes cannot continue to appreciate any further because then no one will be able to afford them. I believe that this is an overly pessimistic vision of the future.

I agree, somewhat, with the philosophy that people should live in their homes rather than expect them to provide great wealth. However, I also believe that there are still a great many opportunities available to people who would like to make money by remodeling and then selling their homes. It may just require a little more effort than was needed during better economic times, but you can still profit from making moderately inexpensive but quality home improvements. In doing so, you also place yourself in a better position for a rebound in the real estate resale market. If history is any indication of the future, and it certainly is, you can expect that better economic days do indeed lie ahead.

Back in Chapter 1, in discussing the extent to which you should remodel, I offered some suggestions that would assist you in determining the direction your neighborhood was headed. By applying these same methods, it may be possible for you to find some excellent home values in growth areas. You should be able to find houses that require making some simple improvements to bring them up to the value of the homes surrounding them. This approach gets back to the time-proven practice of buying the worst house in the best neighborhood. It also relates to the old saying that warns: "The three most important considerations when looking to buy a home are location, location, and location."

Although some of us look forward to the challenges associated with undertaking a remodeling project, many people still want to buy a home in "move in" condition. These people have absolutely no inclination to take on any remodeling whatsoever. They are looking for homes where more recent "quality improvements" and upgrades have already been made. They are often looking for three or more bedrooms, at least two bathrooms plus a half bath or "powder room," excellent kitchens with built-in appliances, plenty of light from good windows and recessed lighting, and extensive closets and storage space.

By sticking to the basics we have discussed throughout the book and by remembering to stay with neutral colors when decorating, you can make a home more appealing to potential buyers even during difficult economic times. The key here lies in doing your homework thoroughly and carefully analyzing the market.

It is also important to remember to design your home remodeling in a manner that is in keeping with the original intrinsic design of the home. The real trick here is in designing improvements in such a fashion that they don't look as if they were added to the original home. To the extent that it is possible, you want people to think that the house was originally built that way. Why do you think this might be important?

There are three types of remodeling additions which I call the "box," the "maze" or "labyrinth," and the "tunnel." The "box" looks exactly as the word implies, as if someone built one and dropped it next to (or on top of) their house. A "maze" or "labyrinth" addition appears to have been added without concern for the smooth passage or flow found throughout the rest of the house. It's easy to lose your way or sense of direction in this type of addition. The "tunnel" appears to extend, or elongate the house on forever. You often have to travel down a long hallway or through a series of rooms to get to the end or to the back of the house.

Have you ever seen these types of additions? Designed to maximize the space, or square footage of a house while minimizing the costs, these remodeling alternatives are not uncommon. They are generally less expensive because they require very little alteration of the existing structure. The problem is that most potential buyers will look at these types of additions and instantly identify them as add-ons. While it is not necessarily a given that this will reduce the value of a home, it may make it harder to sell.

People want to buy homes which make them feel comfortable throughout. They don't want to have to live with the previous owners' poorly designed, cost-cutting alterations. With very little additional expense and effort, you can give greater thought to designing your additions as if they were part of the original designer's master plan. This should pay off when it comes time to sell your home.

When weighing the prospect of embarking on another project for fun and profit, remember to review the discussion earlier in this chapter regarding the tax issues. Take time to look over this book again before you consider taking on a new home remodeling project. Good luck to you!

REVIEW

- Improvements are not tax deductible.

- Capital improvements can be added to the cost basis of your home; repairs cannot.

- Cost basis is defined as the price you paid for your home plus any capital improvements.

- Consider the opportunities available to postpone the capital gains on the sale of your principal residence.

- Consider applying the one-time exclusion of up to $125,000 if you are over 55 and otherwise eligible.

- Save all your home improvement receipts.

- Do not include the cost of your time when calculating home improvement costs for tax purposes.

- Don't sell your new home for at least two years if you plan on further postponing the taxable gain.

- Postpone needed repairs to within 90 days of the sale of your home.

- To postpone the taxable gain on the sale of your home, always buy or build a new home for an amount greater than or equal to the adjusted sales price of your old home.

- Consider borrowing the maximum affordable amount against your new home and save your sale proceeds from the old one for better investment potential.

- Compare your projected estimates with the actual amounts spent to determine savings.

- Consider buying and remodeling another home for fun and profit, but do your homework first.

- Design your remodeling to be in keeping with the original intrinsic design of the home.

Appendix A
Related Associations

American Institute of Architects (AIA)
1735 New York Avenue NW
Washington, DC 20006
(202) 626-7300
(Publishes, among other things, standardized construction contract forms)

American Society of Interior Designers (ASID)
608 Massachusetts Avenue NE
Washington, DC 20002
(202) 546-3480

Home Improvement Research Institute (HIRI)
400 Knightsbridge Parkway
Lincolnshire, IL 60069
(708) 634-4368

National Asbestos Council (NAC)
1777 NE Expressway
Suite 150
Atlanta, GA 30329
(404) 633-2622

National Association of Home Builders of the United States (NAHB)
15th and M Streets NW
Washington, DC 20005
(202) 822-0200
(Publisher of *Builder Magazine*)

National Association of the Remodeling Industry (NARI)
1901 N. Moore Street
Suite 808
Arlington, VA 22209
(703) 276-7600

Appendix B
Major Credit Reporting Agencies

Equifax Information Service Center
Wildwood Plaza
7200 Windy Hill Road, Suite 500
Marietta, GA 30067
Toll Free (800) 685-1111

Trans Union Corporation
PO Box 7000
North Olmstead, Ohio 44070
(Corporate offices are located in Chicago; dial (312) 645-0012 for general information and (312) 645-6000 for information on how to obtain a copy of your credit report.)

TRW Credit Data/Consumer Assistance
PO Box 749029
Dallas, Texas 75374-0000
(214) 235-1200

Appendix C
Related Reference Guides

The following books are available at your local library or by contacting the publishers directly.

The Blue Book Contractors Building and Construction Register
    Published regionally and contains a classified list of general contractors, subcontractors, architects, and engineers, along with material and equipment dealers and manufacturers.
    Published by Contractors Register, Inc.
    30 Undercliff Avenue
    Elmsford, NY 10523
    Toll Free (800) 431-2584; in New York (914) 592-8200

Directory of California Licensed Contractors
    Published by *Building News™*, which also publishes other useful building and construction-related forms.

(In the West)   (In the Northeast)
3055 Overland Avenue   77 Wexford Street
Los Angeles, CA 90034   Needham Heights, MA 02194
(213) 202-7775   (617) 455-1466

Sweet's Catalog File
Products for general building and renovation
Published by McGraw-Hill
Sweet's Group
Attn: Direct Marketing Department–20th Floor
1221 Avenue of the Americas
New York, NY 10020
Toll Free (800) 992-0535

Appendix D
State Agencies for Building Code Standards

The following list includes some state agencies responsible for establishing and enforcing construction standards, building material requirements, and standards of occupancy for buildings in their respective states. Certain states have no agency for this purpose, so other agencies that may provide related information are listed instead. Most county and local governments have established their own building code standards and restrictions; be sure and check with them as well.

ALABAMA
  Building Commission
  800 S. McDonough Street
  Montgomery, AL 36104
  (205) 242-4082

ARIZONA
  Register of Contractors
  800 W. Washington
  Phoenix, AZ 85007
  (602) 542-1502

ARKANSAS
   Contractor's Licensing Board
   621 E. Capitol
   Little Rock, AR 72202
   (501) 372-4661

CALIFORNIA
   Division of Codes and
      Standards
   Housing and Community
      Development Department
   6007 Folson Boulevard,
      Suite A
   Sacramento, CA 95819
   (916) 445-9471

COLORADO
   Division of Housing
   Department of Local Affairs
   1313 Sherman Street
   Denver, CO 80203
   (303) 866-2033

CONNECTICUT
   Department of Public Safety
   294 Colony Street, Building 3
   Meridian, CT 06450
   (203) 238-0611

DISTRICT OF COLUMBIA
   Building and Land
      Regulation Administration
   Construction and Regulatory
      Affairs Department
   614 H Street, NW, Room 312
   Washington, DC 20001
   (202) 727-7340

FLORIDA
   Codes and Standards Section
   Rhyne Building
   2740 Centerview Drive
   Tallahassee, FL 32399
   (904) 487-1824

GEORGIA
   Georgia Building Authority
   1 Martin Luther King, Jr.
      Drive
   Atlanta, GA 30334
   (404) 656-3250

IDAHO
   Building Division
   Labor and Industrial Services
      Department
   317 Main Street
   Boise, ID 83720
   (208) 334-3950

ILLINOIS
   Housing Development
      Authority
   401 N. Michigan Avenue
   Chicago, IL 60611
   (312) 836-5200

INDIANA
   State Building Inspector
   1099 N. Meridian Street,
      Suite 900
   Indianapolis, IN 46204
   (317) 232-1404

IOWA
Building Code Commissioner
Department of Public Safety
Wallace State Office Building
Des Moines, IA 50319
(515) 281-5821

KANSAS
Division of Architectural
Services
Department of
Administration
625 Polk Street
Topeka, KS 66603
(913) 233-9367

KENTUCKY
Housing, Buildings and
Construction
The 127 Building
U.S. 127 S
Frankfort, KY 40601
(502) 564-8044

LOUISIANA
Facility Planning Office
Division of Administration
PO Box 94095
Baton Rouge, LA 70804
(504) 342-0820

MARYLAND
Building Codes and
Administration
Economic and Community
Development Department
45 Calvert Street
Annapolis, MD 21401
(301) 974-2701

MASSACHUSETTS
Building Inspections
1 Ashburton Place,
Room 1301
Boston, MA 02108
(617) 727-7551

MICHIGAN
Bureau of Construction
Codes
Department of Labor
7150 Harris Drive
Box 30015
Lansing, MI 48909
(517) 322-1705

MINNESOTA
Building Code and Standards
Division
Department of
Administration
408 Metro Square Building
St. Paul, MN 55101
(612) 296-4639

MISSISSIPPI
Division of General Services
Department of Finance and
Administration
1501 Sillers Building
Jackson, MS 39201
(601) 359-3621

MISSOURI
Division of Designs and
Construction
PO Box 809
Jefferson City, MO 65102
(314) 751-4174

MONTANA
    Building Codes Bureau
    Department of Commerce
    State Capitol
    Helena, MT 59620
    (406) 444-3933

NEVADA
    State Contractors Board
    70 Linden Street
    Reno, NV 89502
    (702) 688-1141

NEW JERSEY
    Division of Housing and
        Development
    Department of Community
        Affairs
    101 S. Broad Street
    Trenton, NJ 08625
    (609) 292-6132

NEW MEXICO
    Construction Industries
        Division
    Regulation and Licensing
        Department
    Bataan Memorial Building
    Santa Fe, NM 87503
    (505) 827-6258

NEW YORK
    Division of Housing and
        Community Renewal
    1 Fordham Plaza
    Bronx, NY 10458
    (212) 519-5800

NORTH CAROLINA
    Engineering Division
    Department of Insurance
    410 N. Boylan Avenue
    Raleigh, NC 27603
    (919) 733-3901

NORTH DAKOTA
    Office of Intergovernmental
        Assistance
    Office of Management and
        Budget
    14th Floor, State Capitol
    600 East Boulevard
    Bismarck, ND 58505
    (701) 224-2094

OHIO
    Department of Industrial
        Relations
    2323 W. Fifth Avenue
    Columbus, OH 43266
    (614) 481-5582

OREGON
    Division of Building Codes
    Department of Commerce
    401 Labor and Industries
        Building
    Salem, OR 97310
    (503) 378-3176

PENNSYLVANIA
    Department of Labor and
        Industry
    Labor and Industry Building
    Room 1529
    Harrisburg, PA 17120
    (717) 787-3323

SOUTH CAROLINA
State Housing Authority
1710 Gervais Street, Suite 300
Columbia, SC 29201
(803) 734-8702

TENNESSEE
Department of Finance and
Administration
James K. Polk Building
17th Floor
Nashville, TN 37219
(615) 741-2388

TEXAS
Department of Commerce
Business Development
Division
PO Box 12728
Austin, TX 78711
(512) 320-9558

UTAH
Division of Design and
Construction
Facilities Construction
Management Department
4110 State Office Building
Salt Lake City, UT 84114
(801) 538-3266

VERMONT
Department of Labor and
Industry
7 Court Street
Montpelier, VT 05602
(802) 828-2286

VIRGINIA
Housing and Community
Development
205 N. Fourth Street
Richmond, VA 23219
(804) 786-1575

WASHINGTON
Building and Construction
Safety Inspection
Department of Labor and
Industries
805 Plum St., SE
Olympia, WA 98504
(206) 753-7455

WEST VIRGINIA
Office of State Fire Marshal
2000 Quarrier Street
Charleston, WV 25305
(304) 348-2191

WISCONSIN
Bureau of Code Development
Industrial Labor and Human
Relations
PO Box 7969
Madison, WI 53707
(608) 266-3080

WYOMING
Structural Safety
Department
Department of Fire
Prevention
Herschler Building, 2E
Cheyenne, WY 82002
(307) 777-7934

Appendix E
Related Building and Construction Code Books

(Northeastern and Eastern Region)

> *BOCA National Building Code*
> Published by the Building Officials and Code Administrators International, Inc. (BOCA)
> > 4051 Flossmoor Road
> > Country Club Hills, IL 60478
> > (708) 799-2300

(Southeastern Region)

> *Standard Building Code*
> Published by the Southern Building Code Congress International (SBCC)
> > 900 Montclair Road
> > Birmingham, AL 35213
> > (205) 591-1853

(Western Region)

Uniform Building Code™
Published by the International Conference of Building Officials (ICBO)
5360 South Workman Mill Road
Whittier, CA 90601
(310) 699-0541

Index

Notes